ABOUT DEEPAK CH

Deepak Chopra, M.D
guished career as writ
is the author of sixteen books and thirty tape series,
including the breakthrough bestsellers *Ageless
Body, Timeless Mind* and *The Seven Spiritual Laws
of Success*. From 1996 he has headed the Chopra
Center for Well Being in La Jolla, California.

ABOUT LEON NACSON

Leon Nacson is a well-established Australian book
publisher, and the founder of the *Planet* newspaper,
a publication that deals with the environment,
healthy lifestyles, and personal development issues.
He has also facilitated seminars and workshops for
Louise L. Hay, Wayne Dyer, Denise Linn, Shakti
Gawain, Deepak Chopra and Stuart Wilde.

BOOKS BY DEEPAK CHOPRA

Creating Health
Return of the Rishi
Quantum Healing
Perfect Health
Unconditional Life
Ageless Body, Timeless Mind
Journey into Healing
Creating Affluence
Perfect Weight
Restful Sleep
The Seven Spiritual Laws of Success
The Return of Merlin
Boundless Energy
Perfect Digestion
The Way of the Wizard
The Path to Love

BOOKS BY LEON NACSON

A Dreamer's Guide to the Galaxy
I Must Be Dreaming
Cards, Stars and Dreams
(co-authored by Matthew Favaloro)
Deepak Chopra's World of Infinite Possibilities
Stuart Wilde's Simply Wilde
Aromatherapy for Lovers & Dreamers
(co-authored by Karen Downes and Judith White)
Aromatherapy for Meditation & Contemplation
(co-authored by Karen Downes and Judith White)

DEEPAK
CHOPRA

How to Live in a World of
Infinite Possibilities

LEON NACSON

RIDER

LONDON · SYDNEY · AUCKLAND · JOHANNESBURG

First published 1998

3 5 7 9 10 8 6 4 2

First published by Random House Australia Pty Ltd.
This edition published in 1998 by Rider,
an imprint of Ebury Press
Random House, 20 Vauxhall Bridge Road, London SW1V 2SA
www.randomhouse.co.uk

Random House Australia (Pty) Limited
20 Alfred Street, Milsons Point, Sydney,
New South Wales 2061, Australia

Random House New Zealand Limited
18 Poland Road, Glenfield,
Auckland 10, New Zealand

Random House South Africa (Pty) Limited
Endulini, 5A Jubilee Road,
Parktown 2193, South Africa

Random House UK Limited Reg. No. 954009

Papers used by Rider are natual, recyclable products made from
wood grown in sustainable forests

Designed by Phil Campbell
Printed and bound in Norway by AIT Trondheim AS

A CIP catalogue record for this book
is available from the British Library

ISBN 0-7126-7001-7

This book gives non-specific, general advice and should not be
relied on as a substitute for proper medical consultation. The
author and publisher cannot accept responsibility for illness arising
out of the failure to seek medical advice from a doctor.

Dedication

To Keith Milne, Colin Papanderas, Tony Malouf, Phil Wade and Gill Wade.

> Some are dead, some
> are living. In my life,
> I have loved you all.

Acknowledgements
Deepak and I would like to express our gratitude to Carol Floyd and Rachel Eldred for researching and editing this book. Their attention to excellence is an inspiration. We'd also like to sincerely thank Margaret Sullivan and Sue Brockhoff of Random House and Sally Moss of White Kite Productions.

Contents

FOREWORD | *by Krishan Chopra*

'They come through you but they don't belong to you. Give them love, but don't give them directions.'

These inspirational words from author Khalil Gibran really struck a chord within me when I first heard them.

My two sons, Deepak and Sanjiv, are each individuals in their own right, and I've always encouraged them to do things their own way. As they were growing up, there were never any secrets between us—we would tell each other everything. Their mother, Pusta, would read to them from the Scriptures and encourage them to talk about what they had heard. She'd tell them to share everything.

Deepak has always had a tendency to take everything literally. One day he found a butterfly in the garden. He was so excited, he wanted to keep it. Taking his mother's advice to heart, he split it in two and shared it with his brother, Sanjiv.

Deepak is our firstborn. He was very bright right from the beginning, and has always been interested in nature. I can remember an occasion on which I had bought tickets for the whole family to attend a musical celebration. Deepak was sitting on the back porch and I said, 'Come along Deepak, we're all ready to go.' He said, 'Daddy, I'm not interested. I'm listening to the birds.' 'But they won't be there for long,' I said, 'the sun is setting.' He answered, 'It doesn't matter, the moon and the stars will come and I will watch them.'

Both my boys were very fond of school and I once told Deepak I would like him to become a doctor. Deepak said, 'I will never become a doctor.' When I asked him why he replied, 'Because you see all the misery.' With that I said, 'You can be anything you want.'

Sanjiv, however, always wanted to be a doctor, and he is now the Director of Clinical Hepatology and a physician for the Gastroenterology Division at Beth Israel Hospital, Boston; he has also written three medical books in his field. I am so proud of him.

From an early age, Deepak was an avid reader and a prolific writer. He ran the school newspaper, and later newsletters. I went to see his principal one day to discuss Deepak's future. The principal said that it was obvious that Deepak should become a writer and journalist. By the time I left the office I was convinced that Deepak would do well in this field. I returned home and told Deepak about the discussion between his principal and I. Deepak was pleased that he could choose his own profession and that I didn't insist that he become a doctor.

A few years later, after Deepak had finished his senior years, he came to me and out of the blue he said, 'Dad, I want to be a doctor.'

I looked at him and said, 'You didn't take Biology in your senior year, or any of the associated sciences, you will have to do an extra year of pre-medical studies.'

Deepak said 'That's fine', and went on to win the All India competition through which only thirty-five candidates are admitted to the leading medical college.

During his years of study, Deepak would come to me and say, over and over, 'My professors always talk about disease; they never talk about health. Why do they do that?' I didn't know.

During medical school, Deepak met and married Rita, and they had two children, Guatama and Mallika. To support his young family during those years, Deepak would complete each long day as a resident doctor, then read the late-night news on the local Delhi radio station right through to the early hours of the morning.

In time, Deepak decided to move to America. He soon became the Chief of Staff at New England Memorial Hospital. Years later he decided he wanted to give up smoking once and for all, and thought that perhaps meditation and the principles of

Ayurvedic medicine might assist him where everything else had failed. And so began the journey that many people throughout the world are familiar with.

Delhi, Christmas 1996

Introduction | *by Leon Nacson*

As I wandered the corridors of the Chopra Center for Well Being in La Jolla, San Diego, I marvelled at the serenity and beauty of my surroundings.

It's hard to describe what you experience the moment you walk in to the Center. It doesn't matter how tired, stressed or agitated you are, you instantly feel calm; it's almost as though you leave all these emotions at the front door as you enter the incredibly nurturing and empowering space.

The whole Center is a redevelopment of an existing building, and the general design is based on an old-world theme. Indoor plants contribute to the picturesque environment, as does the outdoor herb garden which produces ingredients for guests' food. Antique furniture has been combined with contemporary furniture, including custom-made mosaic tables, evoking the cosmopolitan flavours of East and West. Antique temple bells and gongs have been used as accents in the offices, and the windows are draped in natural linen and gauze-like fabric hanging from iron rods.

The building is a veritable oasis with many delightful additions, including an indoor fountain featuring an elephant head, beautiful chandeliers and a hand-painted mural of the universe. The special Quantum Soup kitchen sits happily in this healthy haven of delight.

It is immediately obvious that the Center is a rejuvenating and harmonious environment in which people can discover their essential nature and recreate not only their lifestyle but the life force within them. Because the human body continually recreates itself through the renewal of cells, the Center emphasises physical regeneration through nutrition, relaxation, meditation, self-discovery and the Ayurvedic principles of living—all of which, together, enable us to redirect old, destructive thought patterns that can ravage mind and spirit.

With expert guidance from those trained in Ayurvedic traditions—fully qualified meditation teachers and trained Ayurvedic medical practitioners—visitors to the Chopra Center for Well Being are examined to identify any established patterns that may be dysfunctional. Programs designed to foster a holistic and balanced approach to life are offered in the most luxurious, peaceful, calm and life-promoting atmosphere. (No wonder I came up with so many great ideas while I was there!)

My tour around the Center took me to the Store of Infinite Possibilities, where all of Deepak's products are on display in the one location, the most popular being his bestselling books.

Over the years just about every notable publisher has asked Deepak to produce a book for them. Consequently, bookshops often cannot stock the full range of his works. Seeing the vast range of his books at the Store started me thinking: wouldn't it be wonderful to produce one book that touched upon all of Deepak's ideas and teachings? What a useful book it would be—almost a mini-resource centre in its own right.

Those of you fortunate enough to know Deepak personally will recognise the routine that follows when you approach him with an idea. He will listen to you, then say, 'I'll get back to you in a couple of weeks.' Twenty minutes later he will be back on the phone with his response and a host of other creative concepts that help the initial idea work faster and more dynamically. And that's exactly what happened when I told him about my idea for this book!

I've been working with Deepak for over ten years and during this time I've had the unique opportunity to question him on all aspects of his philosophy. Most of the information I have collected in this way has been featured in the *Planet*, a healthy-lifestyle, environmental and personal-growth newspaper that I publish in Australia. I recently scanned the *Planet* files and found an abundance of creative and thoughtful information shared by Deepak Chopra. This looked like the perfect basis for the book I had in mind.

I've had the privilege of experiencing Deepak's creativity in many different ways over time. Perhaps the most entertaining and exhilarating way has been through his seminars and workshops. I've travelled with him to some of the most exotic locations in the world, meeting the countless thousands of people who have delighted in his work and attended these events. Having seen the response Deepak's personal presence inspires, I dreamed of producing a book that would give readers a sense of being with him, of hearing his voice.

There is no doubt that Deepak Chopra has a profound message to impart to us all. He has researched and written on a vast range of subjects—from Ayurvedic medicine to meditation, karma to creation, purpose to potential, stress to success—all from the perspective of a fully qualified physician, endocrinologist and quantum healer.

Where was I going to start my 'Pocket Chopra', with so many areas to choose from? I decided the best place to start was at the beginning, right back in the early days when I began to facilitate Deepak's visits and publish interviews in the *Planet*. I quickly realised, with all this information, that I would have to be selective; otherwise I was going to end up with a book the size of a semi-trailer or, to use the analogy of a child loose in a candy store, a big tummy ache.

I decided to structure the book around fundamental questions: questions that would bring out the basic premises on which Deepak's views on healing and expanding our human consciousness are founded. So I headed towards a delicious assortment of chocolaty treats. Like chocolate for most of us, human potential is for Deepak a rich and much-loved subject, something he has been avidly studying and promoting for many years.

With Deepak's training in medicine, it was natural that the book should also address the subject of healing. Although Deepak is an endocrinologist, the science of Ayurvedic medicine and healing through natural forces has been at the forefront of his research into total well-being.

Deepak believes that the body is its own pharmacy. It makes its own drugs—sleeping aids, tranquillisers, and pain relievers. He also teaches that our five senses—hearing, seeing, tasting, smelling and touching—are the gateway to this pharmacy. (Deepak's philosophy and work on healing were the catalyst for the creation of the Chopra Center for Well Being.)

Most of us are conditioned to live within the constraints of a physical world in which we not only deny our inner power to create a life of total well-being—with peace, harmony, love, joy and abundance—but also often ignore our innate ability to heal ourselves or prevent disease in the first place. Too often we rely on conventional medicine and 'scientific' evidence to assess our health, rather than looking at wellness from an individual, holistic perspective.

Deepak says that Western medicine uses its intelligence to treat the immediate problem, but forgets the wisdom and therefore the possibility of preventing the same or similar problems later on. This is where Ayurvedic medicine comes in.

Deepak notes that, in Western medicine, a doctor asks the patient, 'What is wrong with you?' Let's suppose I actually did visit that candy store and eat everything in sight. I would reply that I had a tummy ache. In the Ayurvedic tradition the doctor asks, 'Who is this person who has something wrong?' I would respond, 'I am Leon Nacson, lover of all things sweet.' The orthodox remedy would tell me to take some antacid powder and lie down. The Ayurvedic remedy would look at the reason I had a frenzy in the sweet shop and address the problem from its root cause.

Ayurvedic medicine is an Indian philosophy that was authored by Rishis or sages over five thousand years ago. The basic notion of Ayurveda is that 'your physical health is the balanced integration of the body, mind and spirit', and the mind's power to control the body's well-being is the pivotal wisdom that Ayurveda spins around. With the help of meditation, healing massages, and the use of 'life-giving' foods and herbs, a personal life force can be harnessed which produces harmony, balance and creativity, and encompasses the whole rather than treating the physical and spiritual as separate phenomena. Deepak's aim to bring the powerful healing effects of Ayurvedic medicine to the West has reached a new pinnacle with the opening of the Chopra Center for Well Being.

I won't list for you the other topics in this book. All will be revealed as you read. What I will say is that all the subjects are addressed at a deep and progressive level. I use the word progressive because once you have understood or have even tasted the wisdom that Deepak imparts you will always look forward.

CHAPTER I | *Who Are You?*

In his workshops Deepak asks his audiences to participate in a mystical experience that is simple yet profound.

After audience members pair themselves up with someone they do not know, Deepak asks each person in the pair to take turns asking the other, at fifteen-second intervals, 'Who are you?'

At first the answers given are egocentric—name, job description and personality traits—that is, the tags we give ourselves. As the questions keep coming, 'Who are you?' becomes more spirit-based. Slowly the concept of 'I'm infinite, I'm immortal, and I'm universal' shines through.

This exercise helps participants shift their awareness and break down certain conceptual boundaries about who they are and what their role is. Once they've started, participants find they could go on indefinitely with answers to the question 'Who are you?' It is a wonderful process and an exciting way to begin this book.

How do we begin to find out who we really are?

Firstly, it is vitally important to understand that the self is boundless. To say the self is boundless is to say that it has no boundaries—that is, no restrictions. This is the first spiritual law: the self is a field of pure potentiality. It is not restricted in any way, but is completely free, and therefore it is full of potentiality. It is not confined in either space or time.

This is all very well theoretically, but what does it mean practically? It means that if you experience yourself as boundless then you become a source of infinite possibilities. What does that exclude? Nothing. If you are indeed a field of infinite possibilities, then every intention, every desire, and every dream that you have had, or have, or will have, you should be able to fulfil, because you are operating from a level of pure potentiality.

It isn't just theoretical. It is practical. What limits us are our limitations, our own self-imposed bondage, our own restrictions. So when you understand this, truly understand, you move from boundaries to freedom, from restrictions to no limitations.

To explain to you *why* the self is boundless, I need to explain three terms: the observer; the process of observing; and the observed. You might substitute the terms seer or knower; the process of seeing or of knowing; and scenery or knowledge.

The observer is the realm of the soul or spirit. I will come back to this, since it holds the answer to your question.

The process of observing is the mind, the intellect and the ego. It is the mind that observes, and observation is undertaken through attention. For example, if you are in a crowded room and you hear your own name spoken, your attention goes straight to the person who spoke it and you ignore the rest of the people in the noisy room. Attention [(or your energy)] is the most important component of observation; the other component is intention, or information. So attention and intention—that is, energy and information—are the process of observation.

The observed—the physical, matter, the world— this is the realm of space/time events. Every material event is a space/time event—something that occupies a location in space and has moments in time. It has a beginning, a middle and an end. Your body started out as a speck of DNA. Food was added to it and it became what it is today. The mind, the intellect and ego: these are events in time but not in space. Emotions, desires, beliefs, self-image, ego, social mask—these are not who you really are. There are so many roles you play, but these are just your social roles. Inside of you are many archetypal energies—teacher, sinner, saint, father, son, mother, daughter, and so on. Can the ego be located? Can you take a concept or belief and examine it under a microscope? No. But thoughts do take place in time. Beliefs have a beginning and an end. Emotions have a beginning and an end. I might feel angry now, but in a few minutes I will feel differently.

And now to answer your question. The observer— the soul or the spirit—exists neither in time nor in space. It is spaceless and timeless, and it is the real you. It has no beginning, no middle and no end. It is immortal and cannot die. Only something with a beginning can die. If it never began, how can it end? Spaceless, timeless, dimensionless—that is you. That is the field of pure potentiality. As consciousness moves within itself, it gives rise to mind and ego, and as that moves, it gives rise to the body and the world. From spacelessness to space, from timelessness to time, from non-dimensionality to dimensions, from unmanifest to complete manifestation.

What about the process of observing and the observed? Are they separate from me? If they are, how do we interact?

The observer, the process of observing and the observed: this trilogy describes the whole world of phenomena. Is anything left out at all? No! Take any phenomenon and you will find that everything is included. Now, the field of pure potentiality must include all of that. The concept to grasp, experientially, is that all of these things are the same thing in different disguises. The world is you, the mind is you, the intellect is you and the body is you. The spirit is the only reality. When we really find that out for our own self, we realise that anything is possible. Let me explain it so you can grasp it a little better. Let's go back to the scenery, the environment—that is, the observed. Due to our materialist conditioning, that is the part that people have the most difficulty with.

When we pick up a rose, how do we describe it? It is red, it has petals, it is different from the chair. Is that its intrinsic nature? Or is it just my way of looking at it? Most people think that we observe its intrinsic nature. That is not right. We see it according to our particular instruments of measurement. For example, if you didn't have the receptors to perceive it as red, you'd see it as black. A bee will experience it as food. A bat will experience it as ultrasound. So what is its real nature? How it is experienced is just a function of receptors. But in reality it is made up of atoms. Atoms are made up of subatomic particles, which are nothing but fluctuations of energy and information.

This is the same thing my body is made up of, the same thing the world is made up of. Everything is made up of energy and information. If we didn't know that for a fact, we wouldn't have modern technology—faxes, cellular phones and silicon chips. Our body is just information in a piece of dust. Everything in creation is information and energy—attention and intention.

No matter how separate things appear, at the quantum level all is connected. That field is your extended body. Each of your cells is a local concentration of information and energy, just as you are a local concentration of energy in the world. As you understand this, the idea of separation will begin to flow away from you. When you realise that you are not a physical body and that you are, in fact, a vast, infinite field of possibilities, then the unbroken flow of intelligence in the universe will be at your disposal.

When you talk about 'the superstition of materialism' are you referring to the fact that material things don't exist as we see them?

Yes, that is correct. Materialism is not a fact, but a superstition. We think there is a material world and that we are bodies in the material world. It isn't that way at all! Thought or consciousness is primary, and the material world is a by-product. Your soul or spirit has information and energy, but at a much more primordial level—that is, in seed form. In every seed, as a Vedic expression says, there is the promise of thousands of forests. Just like an oak seed contains an oak tree in seed form, so in the soul or spirit there is the promise of everything that exists in the universe.

Do a thought experiment. Feel the softness of the skin on your arm. Feel the hardness of the bone under the skin. How would you see your arm through a high-powered microscope? You would see a collection of individual cells, loosely bound together by connective tissue. Each cell is a watery bag of protein, a chain of molecules held together by invisible bonds. If you used an even more powerful microscope, you would see separate atoms of carbon, hydrogen and so on. Go even closer and you would arrive at the boundaries between matter and energy: you wouldn't see 'things' but whirling electrons dancing around a nuclear core. What you thought was solid matter is just an energy trail. At this level there is nothing substantial to be touched or seen.

Let's look even deeper into quantum space where all light disappears and is replaced by darkness. Now you are where space and time have disappeared. There is no such thing as before or after: no concept of big or small. Now, you might realise that in reality these terms are meaningless, for you have arrived at the womb of the universe. You are everywhere and nowhere. However, do you think that your leg or your body has ceased to be? No, why would it? Did you go anywhere? You body still exists on all those levels. Each of these levels is a layer of transformation.

I have said many times that the five senses are a mirage. Matter is 99.9 per cent empty space. The void between two electrons is proportionately that of the space between galaxies. If you look deep enough into the fabric of matter and energy you will arrive at the origin of the universe.

What makes us have particular thoughts?

There is a statistical likelihood of a specific thought occurring, given a specific situation. For example, I might look at the weather getting cold and overcast and think, 'Maybe I should go to Florida', because I don't like cold weather. But you might think, 'Oh, great! Maybe we'll get some snow and I'll go skiing.' Someone else might look forward to a cosy night in front of a fire. There are hundreds of possible reactions, but there are probabilities that certain people will think certain thoughts. I call this a probability amplitude to the field of infinite possibilities in the gap. This probability amplitude defines the statistical likelihood of the next thought. When you know someone really well, you'll be able to guess what their next thought is.

What defines the probability amplitude?

In Vedic literature it is called karma. Karma simply means experience or action—that is, action that creates experience. If I wash my clothes, that is karma. It is action, experience. What does karma do? It creates memory, or, in Sanskrit, *samskara*. What does memory do? It creates the possibility of desire. If I go into a coffee shop and smell the aroma of coffee beans, I might want a cappuccino [because I have had one before, and remember how it smelled]. In Sanskrit this desire is called *wasana*. Desire creates action, or the possibility of action.

This cycle of karma, *samskara* and *wasana* is what I call the 'software of the gap'. Even though the gap is silent, it is not an empty silence. On the contrary, it is pregnant with possibility. This possibility has probability built into it, and defining that are karma, *samskara* and *wasana*. You and I are different because we've had different experiences in our past. We've metabolised every little bit of experience, and our experience has created the software of our souls. To be completely free, we have to be free of karma.

Is memory just our own, personal, faulty recall?

Memories, which are based on karma, are both personal and impersonal. Personal memories are things that we experienced: I did that, or I went there, and so on. They go back to our childhood, and even to our intra-uterine life, to our conception and beyond. Because the soul cannot be squeezed into the volume of one body or the span of one lifetime, our memories go back eons of time, into other lifetimes.

We also have holographic memories. Beyond our personal memories are impersonal memories, memories of our race. Beyond that there are memories of our species. Beyond that are memories of other species. Beyond that are memories of everything in this universe. Beyond that are memories of the source.

When you say 'the source' are you referring to God?

You can use whatever term you want for this source—God, or whatever. How do you spell God? G-O-D. It is very interesting: generation, organisation and destruction. That which creates, that which organises, that which gets rid of—the quantum field of life. This body is regenerating all the time, replacing its atoms every year. Right in your being is the whole universe. I am the universe. In microcosm I have access to it. I don't need to struggle, just to remember. And I remember by going beyond my superficial memories. If I can then go beyond that, I have access to the software that runs the machinery of the universe. All of the phrases that mean God also mean 'I am the universe'. You return to the memory of who you really are.

Can you explain the idea of holographic memories?

The body is a holographic manifestation of memory. A hologram is a three-dimensional projection of memory. If you want to make a hologram of something, you take a laser beam—a beam of light that is coherent (that is, every bit of the beam is vibrating at the same frequency)—and put it through a beam splitter. One part is called the 'object beam', the other part is called the 'reference beam'. The object beam hits the object. The reference beam hits a mirror, bounces off and interferes with the object beam to create what is called an interference pattern. This interference pattern can be recorded on a photographic plate, and it appears to be just scribbles. If you pass a laser beam through this, you get a three-dimensional projection of the original object in space and time. If it is well made, you cannot tell the difference between me and my hologram. It is very much like the original. Now, the most magical thing about this hologram is this: if you cut it with scissors into trillions of bits, and take the tiniest bit of it, and put a laser beam through it, you will get all of me again. That is the very reason it is called a hologram, because the whole is contained in every part.

The universe is also a holographic universe. William Blake wrote:

To see the whole world in a grain of sand,
heaven in a wildflower,
to hold infinity in the palm of your hand
and eternity in an hour

This is a holographic description. The Vedic expression says, 'In Indra's Heaven there is a set of pearls so contained; pick up one of them and you'll see all of them'. That is holographic as well. What you see out there is actually a holographic tape. It is the quantum soup, churning within itself, and produces the world when in conjunction with an observer. Each cell in your body represents the entire universe of memory. The mechanics of the creation of the entire universe is within each of those cells. We also have personal memories. But even our personal memories are shared memories, many of them. Your five senses are, quite literally, the reference beams in the interference pattern in the subtle body [(a combination of the mind, the intellect and the ego)]. We have a subtle body with all five senses as intention; that is, you can imagine music, sight or smell. We visualise when we introduce the intention. I like to say, as we go within our own physical body, that we are eavesdropping on the cosmic mind, for our mind is a holographic representation of the cosmic mind. You don't have to go outside to find the nature of anything—it is right here [within you]—each of us is the universe in microcosm. In the Vedic tradition, the phrase is: 'As is the atom, so is the universe.' In other words: as is the microcosm, so is the macrocosm. As is the human body, so is the cosmic body. As is the human mind, so is the cosmic mind.

Do we need to be free of desire, too?

You don't need to be free of desire, but free of restrictions in desire. Desire is the connection between the existent and the non-existent, according to the Rig Veda. We always hear that desire is a bad thing. But the universe is created through desire.

What about the notion of chaos. Is it possible to avoid chaos in our lives?

Why would you want to? Nietzsche once wrote, 'You must have chaos within you to give birth to a dancing star.' I really believe once you're comfortable with the turbulence within you, that's the beginning of the source of creativity. I call this process 'divine discontent'. If you didn't have it, you'd be bored and you wouldn't create anything.

Turbulence and chaos are actually the beginnings of order. I say to all those people out there who are uncomfortable with their uncertainty, with their confusion, with their turbulence, to be grateful for this astounding, lucid confusion because it's the birthplace of infinite creativity. The option is to be the prisoner of the known, and the known is nothing other than the prison of the past. It's also the prison of other people's values, of what things should be like.

How do we know that we are 'a field of infinite possibilities'?

If you consult the world's spiritual literature—the Bible, the Koran, and so on—you will find this expression: 'You are in this world, but not of this world.' What does it mean?

Every memory is an interpretation, every desire is a choice. The real you is therefore someone who makes an interpretation or a choice. There are only a few kinds of thoughts: interpretations and choices, memories, and desires. There are no other kinds of thoughts. Thoughts are born of karma. Every thought you have has your entire karmic history embedded in it. Every thought makes it necessary to have another thought. Thoughts may seem to be so fleeting. But each contains your entire karmic history, since the beginning of time. Your last thought before death contains your total karmic history.

Although we have technologies today that are so sophisticated that they enable us to watch a sugar molecule or particle make its way to the brain, or even to see the effects of a flicker of a thought a microsecond after we have it, we can't find the 'person' in the body or the brain. (For example, this person who is writing these words is not in the body or the brain.) Why can't we find it? Because it isn't *in* the brain.

The field of pure possibility occurs in the gap between our thoughts. It is in this gap that the transition from non-local to local occurs, from boundless to boundaries. Thoughts are like lightning. But in between my thoughts is the 'me' who is having the thoughts. Therefore the real you, the thinker of the thought, is in the space between your thoughts. This space is silent, and it is a field of infinite possibilities. Why? Where is the thought 'lemon' before you have it? It is in the field of infinite possibilities, which is non-local reality.

When you examine this non-local reality, you see that the observed is local, the process of observation is partially local, but that the observer is not local. The real person who is reading this book is non-local. You can't find this person anywhere. Where does it exist? You can point to a body, you can observe a thought, but you can't observe your self. Your self is nowhere and everywhere at the same time. Non-local becomes local, through the gap.

In practical terms what does all this mean?

If attention and intention are the two components of observation, or consciousness, which we have seen, it stands to reason that if you master them, you can master anything. It is very simple. People think it must be complex: don't be misled, because it is so simple. Your breath is the junction between mind and body. It connects mind to body. Even though mind and body are part of the same continuum, we experience them as different, and the breath connects them. The breath mirrors the movement of consciousness. We know that, even superficially, when we are anxious, our breathing is irregular. When we say something is breathtaking, we mean that it does literally make us stop breathing. Beauty, for instance, takes us beyond the mind and body.

The link to our mastery of all is through the gaps between thoughts, but this link can get old and rusty, even though it is always there.

What is it that makes this link deteriorate?

What makes it 'old and rusty' is the turbulence of our internal dialogue which gets caught up with trivial and mundane concerns of everyday lives. We focus our energies on getting approval, on achieving control, on justifying our actions, or on other things. Then the magic of our existence disappears. Our existence becomes boring and sad. But we can restore the magic by finding out who we are. The magic is always there; we just need to rediscover it.

Sex obviously plays a role in the process of discovering who we are. Is there a relationship between spirituality and sex?

Yes, sexuality is one of the most obvious examples of spirituality itself. Sex *is* spirituality because flesh and spirit are not two separate entities. Sex is not just a connection of flesh to flesh, it is a connection of spirit to spirit. Sexual energy is the creative energy of the universe. Anything that is alive is alive because of that energy.

We as humans have the capacity to be creative at all levels, from the biological to the spiritual. Sex is creative when it gives us the experience of a new feeling, a new insight, a new knowing that is about us and another person. Whenever we feel a connection towards anything—art, music, poetry or science; whenever we experience passion; whenever we are inspired; whenever we have insight; whenever we feel excited, enthusiastic, energised or creative—we can be sure that sexual energy is at work.

The experience of sex allows us to go beyond the mini-self of the ego, and it is therefore the only form of meditation for many people.

Orgasm is a good example of a peak experience, so when you look at the characteristics of that experience, you'll find the following: loss of ego, naturalness, a sense of timelessness, surrender, loss of defensiveness, loss of vigilance, and communion. You can see that that is a spiritual experience. It's an experience of unity consciousness where the lover and the beloved become one, and the spiritual experience is indeed that experience of unity consciousness in which the observer and the observed become one. Orgasm gives us a brief glimpse of what unity consciousness is, and it's a temporary state of liberation. But if you understand the mechanics of it, then you can see that sexuality can give us insight into what it could be like to be in a permanent state of liberation.

Any distinction between sex being profane and spirituality being sacred is an artificial one. In fact, in the Eastern wisdom traditions, sex has been used as a means to get close to God because it brings you closer to your primordial state of ecstatic energy, which is where God is.

What is love?

Love is spirit, love is the ultimate truth at the heart

of creation. Love is the unifying force of nature. Love connects everything to everything else, and it's the only motivation for doing anything—even when people do harmful things. If people go beyond their superficial motivation, they will see that they are doing it because they want to be loved.

In your book The Path to Love, *you talk about seven different levels of 'love'. Can you outline what they are?*

The Path to Love explores the seven steps of our soul's transformation and it moves from separation into unity. The first step or stage is attraction—what makes certain people attractive and what makes other people unattractive. This boils down to the fact that those who are attracted to others are comfortable with themselves, they are comfortable with their own ambiguity, with their shadow as well [as their solid self]. They are comfortable with the fact that having strong and weak points does not make them flawed; it makes them complete. People who are not attracted to others are not attractive to themselves either. They are constantly comparing themselves with others and looking for approval from others. They have a passive attitude to life and they're very selective in the way they display their love, in that they will give great importance to certain people and ignore other people altogether. On the other hand, those who feel attractive to themselves, and are therefore attracted to others, are those who have relinquished their need to judge. These people are those who do not depend on others to feel attractive or to feel loved, those who believe deep down that they are lovable and therefore attractive, those who do not expect anything in return for being loving and who are giving at all levels.

After that comes the second stage, that of infatuation. In the stage of infatuation, we go beyond the ego. In fact, infatuation is also a temporary state of liberation because you start seeing another person almost as a divine being whom you worship, and during infatuation you get the experience of transcendence.

The third stage is communion. After the initial excitement of infatuation, familarity sets in, and with familarity the return of ego and its need to control. This is an important stage, for it decides whether the relationship will flower and mature, or break apart. It will break apart if both people involved in the relationship choose to build up defences, and it will mature and flower if they share their differences. At this stage, therefore, the three most important things are equality, sensitivity and communication. Equality in spirit, no matter what our social status, or our financial status, might be. Sensitivity, which means the ability to know how another person is feeling, and also know all the paradoxes that go along with that. And communication—the ability to willingly let someone else know of our deepest fears about ourselves. If communion succeeds, it leads to intimacy.

Intimacy and sexuality are quite closely related. When spiritual fulfilment, physical fulfilment and erotic flowering all merge, then the experience is very sacred, very intimate and very sexual, and if this stage matures it leads to the next stage, which is surrender and non-attachment.

This is a very important stage because now the temporary stage of liberation that was experienced in intimacy tends to become more permanent. Yet that experience of timelessness and spiritual presence can only come when we learn to be non-attached and to surrender. Surrendering means that we never feel the need to deny, manipulate, control, convince, cajole, insist, beg or seduce; we simply allow, and in that allowing we let love flow and work its miracles. At this stage, you can begin to go beyond reactions into creativity and awareness. This is the stage which allows us to experience intuition, and beyond intuition, the visionary and sacred responses.

The state of surrender and non-attachment lead on to the sixth stage, the stage of passion. Elsewhere I've dealt with passion in spiritual terms as the two energies, male and female. Shiva is usually referred to as the male energy, and it has five aspects. These are creation, protection, destruction, concealment, and revealment or revelation. The female energy is often referred to as Shakti, and it also has five components. These are pure consciousness, pure awareness, bliss, desire, knowledge and action. There are ten different archetypal energies that are responsible for keeping the flame of the soul alive, and when that flame of the soul is kept alive, then we have passion, not only for our relationships but a passion for life itself.

This kind of passion ultimately leads to the final stage of love, the stage of ecstasy. And there are three kinds of ecstatic experience. The first is physical ecstasy—that is, sensual delight carried to its ulitmate. Physical ecstasy occurs in sexuality, or in any sensual experience—any experience with nature. The second type of ecstasy is archetypal or mythical ecstasy. An understanding of this is very imporant because it meets the turbulence of our daily activity. Our unconscious motivations lie in the mythical world. Inside us are our primal gods and goddesses, and these gods and goddesses want to be born. We know this without knowing it, in that we act upon our mythical world without bringing these beings into our conscious awareness. In mythical terms then, ecstasy is a sacred journey into the underworld as unconscious, which is portrayed in countless myths. We have lost this mythical experience of ecstasy primarily because our intention has become so caught up with the trivial and mundane things in life. We need to restore a new mythology for our age. I personally believe that this is essential if we are to restore the experience of ecstasy. And the final type of ecstasy is the sacred kind of ecstasy, the spiritual ecstasy which is really going into higher states of consciousness, from cosmic consciousness to God consciousness to illumination consciousness. I feel that *The Path to Love* is my most important book so far because it outlines a path that has been trodden by many wise traditions throughout the world, and it lays out the signposts along the path—attraction, infatuation, communion, intimacy, surrender and non-attachment, passion and ecstasy.

CHAPTER 2 | *What Are You Doing Here?*

Flicking through past issues of the *Planet,* I noticed that we had published many articles on Deepak, and in response to these articles we always received an influx of letters from our readers asking us questions about Deepak's work. Reading through these letters again, I realised that the same questions were being asked over and over, and they all boiled down to the fundamental issue 'What am I doing here?'

In this chapter, I thought it would be great to quote some of these questions and ask Deepak for the answers personally.

What I love about Deepak's work is that it enables you to go deep within, but it also reminds you not to forget the surface. In other words, there should be a balance between spiritual contemplation and physical motivation.

*The soul is beyond this space/time continuum,
but while I am in time-bound consciousness will I
ever experience the truth?*

You say 'while I am in time-bound consciousness'
as if you know where you are. I am trying to tell
you that who you really are is not in time-bound
consciousness. If you are looking for the soul, and
you say 'where is it?', you are asking the wrong
question. You are trying to find something in space
and time that is spaceless and timeless. And yet it is
you. The best way to access this is in the gaps
between our thoughts. In the space between these
thought is the thinker of the thoughts. And this is
the silent field of infinite possibilities.

What is thought and where does it come from?

That is an interesting and fundamental question. In
our everyday thinking, we regard thoughts as less
real than physical objects. But we have already
talked about the superstition of materialism, and I
think I've demonstrated that when you examine
physicality on a quantum level, and if you look
deep enough into the fabric of matter and energy,
you will arrive at the origin of the universe. All
things, all events, have a common source outside
our everyday reality. Now consider this: is it possible,
do you think, that a thought has the same source of
creation as a galaxy of stars or a cluster of nebulae,
or a rainforest, or a human body?

Are you saying that we can examine thoughts just as we examine a physical object, and that we can go back to its source?

That is a pretty good way of putting it. Thought is a quantum event. A physicist would define a quantum event as the 'smallest indivisible unit in which waves of information and energy are either emitted or absorbed'. A quantum of light, for example, is a photon. Electrical quantum events are electrons, and someone has called the as-yet-undiscovered quantum of gravity a graviton. These are labels for defining units of energy and information. A thought is fleeting, unpredictable and invisible. So are all quantum events. A thought, like a quantum event, is a unit of information and energy. Quantum events create the manifest universe and the manifest body. Thoughts transform themselves into space/time events that we call matter.

Thoughts transform themselves into matter? How?

I can see that you are thinking that this is just a speculation drawn from Eastern philosophy. But this 'Eastern philosophy' also has its basis in science. This fact—that there are biochemical substrata to the thinking process—has been known for about fifteen years. Emotions, feelings and memories transform themselves into biochemical events, or neuropeptides. They are biochemical messengers from inner space. Brain cells communicate with each other through them. There are receptors for peptides not only in brain cells but in all the cells of the body. For example, immune cells, which protect you from disease, have these receptor sites for the same neuropeptides that are produced in the brain as a result of thought and feeling and emotion. So these immune cells are constantly eavesdropping on your thoughts. In fact, there is no difference between the nervous system and the immune system; the immune system is simply a circulating nervous system. Any neurobiologist will tell you this. But it isn't just the immune cells that have this capability, but other cells in our bodies. So, when you say I have a gut feeling about something, this is not a metaphor. What I am saying is that this body, made up of molecules, is the objective experience of consciousness, and that the mind is the subjective experience of consciousness.

What is the real difference between objective and subjective?

Nothing. The two are inseparable, immutably bound together. They are the same phenomenon in different guises. They are both information and energy. We just experience thoughts subjectively as our mind. We experience it objectively as our body and as the physical world. Our sensors are transducers: they translate information and energy into taste, texture, form and colour. In our minds, we experience that quantum soup as thoughts. But it is all the same thing. There is a wonderful, ancient saying in Vedic literature that sums it up: 'I am that, you are that, all this is that, and that is all there is.'

I think about me being the thinker of the thought, and about you being the thinker of the thought, and how this thinker is the field of infinite possibilities. Are there lots of such fields? If so, how can this field of infinite possibilities, or the soul, or God, or whatever we call it, be absolute?

Is it possible that there is only one thinker? That you and I are one? That the distinctions that set us are apart are not absolute distinctions, but distinctions created in space and time, and that arise due to ignorance of our true nature?

I can see why you are confused, and to clear up your confusion I need to explain the mechanics of the continuum from the field of infinite possibilities to the physical body.

We have the physical body, and we can call the physical universe around us the extended body. Then we have the subtle body, with its three layers; mind, intellect and ego. In the mind we experience emotions and desires; the intellect is the domain of ideas, concepts and beliefs. Ego is the totality of object referral. Ego is our self-image. It is ourselves seen through the eyes of others. It is our social mind. It is social mask that we wear, the role we play. When you are introducing yourself, you don't say, 'I am a holographic representation of the universe that is manifesting as a continual space-time event in the probability amplitude that comes out of a field of infinite possibilities', do you? That might be the most accurate thing you can say about yourself, but you are more likely to say, 'Hello, I am John So-and-So. I am the manager of the local bank.' In the Vedic scriptures, this is called 'the mistake of the intellect'. We sacrifice the self for self-image, the spirit for the ego. This sacrifice is just another word for the birth of time. The best definition of time is that it is 'the continuity of memory that uses the ego as its internal reference point'. That is the ego, part of the subtle body, and it is the ego that transforms itself into ideas and concepts. The ideas and concepts transform themselves into desires and emotions. Desires and emotions transform themselves into patterns of energy, and these patterns of energy transform themselves into molecules, and these molecules transform themselves into the experience of the world, as we discussed earlier.

Beyond the subtle body is the soul, which we also call the causal body. In the soul is the probability amplitude continuum. The probability amplitude is affected by karma, memory and desire, which I have described as the 'software of the soul'. This soul still partakes of individuality, because it has probability amplitude. Beyond the soul lies the field of infinite possibilities, or eternal possibility. Our space- and time-bound identities are like ripples in that vast ocean of consciousness. Everything comes from this ultimate ground of creation—the ground of creation of everything else.

So there are three levels, and at every level a different aspect of yourself dominates. You know about the continuum that comprises the observer, the process of observation, and the observed. All are present at every level, but they are unmanifest at different levels. At the level of soul, of causal body, the observer dominates the experience. At the level of the subtle body, the ego and mind, the process of observation dominates. And at the level of the physical body, the observed dominates.

Although each person seems separate and independent, we are connected to the patterns of intelligence that govern the whole cosmos. You think you are a person, and that I am a person, and that we are separate. We lose our separation as we descend from physical being to soul, and there is no separation at all in the field of infinite possibilities. Like a wave temporarily thrown up out of the ocean, we experience separation, but when the wave motion abates, there is no separation. Buddha said, 'This lifetime of ours is like a flash of lightning in the sky', and he described life to be 'as transient as autumn cloud'. Although we seem to be separate, we are not. It is as the great American poet Walt Whitman said: 'Every atom belonging to you belongs to me.'

I understand the 'how' of it all, but I am still puzzled by the 'why'. Why does separation occur?

You might remember that the 'why' question occurs only in space and time, and implies that there is a specific cause to every event. Yet everything is as it is because the universe is as it is. But creation is intelligence. We are conscious beings in a conscious universe, and through you and me, the universe becomes conscious of itself. That is the privilege we have as humans. To watch the birth and death of beings is like watching the movements of a dance. A lifetime rushes by like a torrent down a steep mountain. We identify with an image of our self instead of our true selves: that is why we get the experience of time. But time does not exist as an absolute, only eternity does. Time is quantified eternity.

The mechanics of creation are nothing other than the self interacting with itself to experience itself as the observer, as the process of observation, and as the observed. The observer, interacting with its own self, creates the process of observation, which creates the world. You are the universe. Curving back within myself, I experience the world, and create it again and again. The purpose of all spiritual seeking is to know that—not to just think it, not to just understand it intellectually, but to know that. You are not in the mind, the mind is in you. You are not in the world, the world is in you.

I am afraid of death, yet you say death is nothing to fear. Can you explain that?

Although the observed and the process of observation are changing, the observer is unchanging. Most of us identify with the process rather than the observer. The observer, your true self, is immortal, silent, non-changing. If your identity comes from that reference point—that is, you identify with the observer rather than with the ego— then you will get rid of all fear. What is fear? We are all afraid of letting go of the known, of letting go of the world. We are attached to the scenery because we identify with the scenery. But the scenery is ever-changing. You change every day. You were a little boy or a little girl, an adolescent, an adult. Which one of these images of yourself is you? The answer is simple: none of them. Let me say it clearly: you are the timeless factor in the midst of time-bound change. Experience is time-bound. It has a beginning, a middle and an end. But the experiencer is timeless. All fear is the fear of mortality in disguise. We fear death, but what are we really fearing? In fact, we are fearing death of the scenery, of the known. But if you are able to let go of the scenery in every moment of your life, then you will never be afraid. All change is just quantified mortality. We know instinctively that what changes cannot be eternal. We also know instinctively that we are beyond change, because we observe change. If you touch that part of yourself that is non-changing, and you make that your anchor, your reference point, your identification, then by and by, there will be nothing to fear.

When you aren't attached to the world, is it still enjoyable?

Much *more* so! If you knew nothing could hurt you, wouldn't you be happier? If you have the knowledge of eternal, unbounded reality, you don't take things seriously. You feel lighthearted, carefree. You have a daily experience of the awesome magnificence of eternity, of infinity, of unbounded reality. When you experience reality, you experience laughter and carefreeness. As I often say, seriousness is a hallmark of the ego. Non-seriousness is a hallmark of the spirit.

Does that mean we shouldn't worry about responsibility?

Be careful here. Don't confuse seriousness with responsibility. Responsibility means the ability to have a response. You can be both lighthearted and responsible. If you are serious, you are not really responsible. On the contrary, you are wallowing in self-pity and self-importance. Seriousness is a sign of self-pity. People go through their lives worrying about things. They worry that they will be rejected; that the weather will spoil their picnic; that their children will suffer. Worrying about things is an anticipation of a response—it is fear-based and ego-based. Spontaneous action is joyful and brings you the experience of the love of life. Rumi said if you have not been a passionate lover, don't count your life as lived.

You have explained karma. But how can we stop the karma that we don't want? How can the process be stopped? What do we do to stop the desires we don't want?

There are two kinds of desires: evolutionary desires and harmful desires. You cannot control them because they are karma. In fact, if you try to control them, it becomes even harder. You cannot *not* think of pink elephants just because someone tells you 'don't think of pink elephants'. You cannot manipulate your thinking process.

So what do we do? Do we just give in to our karma?

As you meditate and go into the gap, the process washes some of the karma off. In fact, every time you meditate, your karmic software changes a little bit. Not radically, but in some little way. So that is the first way around karma.

There are two other ways. The second way is to pay off your karmic debt. In fact, that is what most people do all the time—we are paying off our karmic debt. Or you might have some karmic credits. Karma is the perfect accounting system: everything balances perfectly. The cosmic computer doesn't break down; it doesn't have software problems; it doesn't need parts replaced.

A third way is to work the negative karma into positive karma. Instead of giving in to your negative karma, just look for the seed of opportunity in your negative karma. Be ever alert to the spiritual lesson you are being taught at every moment in your life.

Beyond these is a technique called sutra practice, which involves actually introducing new software into the gap. 'Sutra' comes from the same root word as suture, to stitch. We stitch the self back together, repair the karma and repair the cosmic software.

Is there free will or determinism?

This is one of the basic questions. My answer is one you might not expect: there is both free will and determinism, simultaneously. If we are in the state of ignorance, or bondage, or unawareness, then we are bound by determinism. If we are in the state of wakefulness, then there is free choice. There is a range. At one end of the spectrum, there is complete determinism, on the other end, free choice. What makes the difference between each notch on the spectrum? The difference is simple: it depends on how awake we are to the spirit. Let me tell you a story. A great sage was dying. He left his body consciously; he even made the choice of when to die. In Sanskrit death is called *maha samadi,* the big meditation. Leaving that way is very elegant, that is style. Anyway, one of his devoted disciples called out as he was dying: 'Who are you? Are you the messiah? Are you God?' 'No,' the sage replied, 'I am none of those things. I am awake. That's all.' So you see, if you are truly awake, you can make the choice to die as you want. You can even incarnate the way you want to.

Do you believe in reincarnation?

People want to know about reincarnation, about out-of-body experiences, but I always say 'think about the mystery of your in-body experience first'. There is nothing supernatural; everything is natural. There are plenty of mysteries now without worrying about future lives, past lives, or other things.

Don't try to imagine past lives. Just use attention and intention. Effortlessness is the key. You will then begin to peel back the layers of your soul to find your spirit. The important thing is to find out who you are. All else will follow out of that.

There are seven things you should remember:

1 Your real nature is spirit. It knows everything there is to know when it needs to know it.

2   Outer reality is always a mirror of inner reality. Inner reality projects itself as outer reality.

3   As we become familiar with the above fact, then even nature will begin to reflect our moods.

4   The spirit is beyond the pulls of experience, which always come in opposing pairs. Up and down, light and dark, joy and sorrow. But the spirit is independent of this scenery of contrasts.

5   The spirit is always awake. The body and mind can go to sleep. In order to know the spirit, you have to be alert to it, to pay attention to its wakefulness.

6   We need solitude in order to befriend the spirit. People are afraid of being alone because they equate it with loneliness. In our society, especially, we seem to feel that if we are alone, then we are not alive. We are almost ashamed of it. But solitude is necessary. In order to know who you are, you need to spend some time with yourself.

7   The spirit knows the secrets of immortality.

CHAPTER 3 | *Body, Mind, Universe*

Most people know that Deepak is a well-respected endocrinologist, and since the early 1980s he has combined his knowledge and skill in this area with his exploration of mind/body medicine. Deepak has thus been instrumental in bringing the enormous benefits of holistic medicine to the attention of the general public.

The son of a prominent cardiologist, Deepak became a physician in New Delhi, India, where he attended the prestigious All India Institute of Medical Sciences. He set his sights on a career in Western medicine and moved to the United States, where he completed studies in internal medicine and endocrinology. He went on to teach at Tufts University and Boston University Schools of Medicine, and before long became chief of staff at New England Memorial Hospital. Uncomfortable with modern medicine's reliance on prescription drugs, Deepak extended his practice to bring together the best of ancient wisdom and modern science.

Recently, Deepak opened the Chopra Center for Well Being in La Jolla, California. The Center is a spiritual, physical, emotional and mental oasis. It offers educational programs and treatments for the integration of mind, body, spirit and environment. Special features of the center include meditation and yoga rooms, a private diningroom, a demonstration kitchen and a theatre-style conference room accommodating up to eighty people. Then there's the Store of Infinite Possibilities, the store that planted the seed in my mind for this book.

I put the following questions to Deepak while I was relaxing in the lounge area of the Center on one of my many visits.

I am puzzled by the idea of mind and matter being one and the same thing. Would this imply that physical health is inseparably connected to your mind?

There are many scientific experiments that demonstrate clearly that mental phenomena affect physiological phenomena. We talked earlier about how immune cells react to your internal dialogue, and that is one discovery in the field of medicine that emerged only in the last few decades. It's called psychoneuroimmunology.

There was an interesting experiment done at the National Institute of Health. A scientist gave mice injections of a chemical called Poly IC, which stimulates the immune system—at least in mice. Experiments showed that when you gave them another experience at the same time—in this case they used the smell of camphor—eventually their immune systems would be stimulated every time they smelt camphor. They confirmed the study by trying the same sort of experience with something that destroys the immune system, and combining injections of that with the taste of saccharine. Soon the mice would start destroying their immune system whenever they tasted saccharine.

What was the cause of this? It was just the interpretation of a memory. It has been estimated that the average human thinks about sixty thousand thoughts a day. We are bundles of conditioned reflexes that are triggered by people and circumstances into predictable outcomes of behaviour and also predictable biochemical reflexes. We become the victims of our own memories, of the stale repetition of outworn memories.

Is there a way in which we can break free of this situation?

If these reflexes are the result of energy and information, and if energy and information are a result of interpretations of memory—or of thought, feeling and emotion—then by witnessing this whole process, we may be able to influence the biochemical and behavioural expressions of energy and information.

I have explained elsewhere that we replace ninety-eight per cent of our bodies each year, so you might wonder why you continue to have the same illnesses. 'Why,' you might say, 'don't I shed my tendency to suffer from migraines when my body is changing all the time?' The answer to that question may be that through karma, through the conditioning of action, which creates the software of our souls, we continue to generate the same impulses of information and energy, and so continue to manifest the same bio-chemical and physiological events, and consequently the same diseases.

If memory, though, causes biochemical events to happen, is there any hope of changing that?

Vedic science, or the science of Ayurveda, comes to us from a very ancient tradition. It says, 'I use my memory but I do not allow memories to use me.' That is a very interesting idea. Obviously, you use memory all the time. You wouldn't keep any of your appointments if you didn't. You wouldn't know who your mother and father were, or how to get home tonight. But if you allow memories to use you, you are in a constant state of reaction.

When we talk about witnessing, detaching, about accessing the gap and thus the software of the soul, we are talking about nothing less than accessing the source where all these conditioned reflexes can be altered. That is what I mean when I talk about freedom and determinism. We are like Pavlovian dogs. If someone tells us we are great, we feel terrific. If someone says something insulting to us, we feel bad. Where is the freedom in that? But if you are aware that you are not the ego, and if your internal reference point shifts to the spirit, then you begin to free yourself from determinism. You are bound by what you identify with, and freedom comes through acknowledging that you are the creator of all this, not the time-bound entity that identifies with the ego.

We seem to experience the world as mind and body, and I can understand now that they are one and the same thing. How does a human being, though, really experience them as one, rather than as separate?

Seeing the world as physical is just a response of the observer. We can liken ourselves to King Midas. He was envied because everything he touched turned to gold. Yet because of this, he couldn't know what a loving caress felt like. We are like that, too—we can never know the true texture of quantum reality because, even as we turn to perceive, we make it material, time-bound and part of the material world. In our time-bound state, we are ignorant of those states of consciousness that seers and sages have talked about since ancient times. One of these sages said, 'Infinite worlds come and go in the vast expanse of my consciousness. They are like motes of dust dancing in a beam of light.' As I've mentioned previously, anyone who has delved into the spiritual literature belonging to the great spiritual movements of the world will find the notion, stated in different ways, of 'We are in the world, but not of it.' The real you is the soul and it is beyond the world.

What is health?

Health is not just the absence of disease but a state of vitality, of energy, of creativity—a higher state of consciousness. You and your physical body, and your subtle body too, are part of the body of the universe. When the intelligence of the universe goes to your body, effortlessly and spontaneously, then you are in a state of health. When for any reason the intelligence of the universe meets resistance, or is blocked, you start to experience discomfort, or disease (dis-ease). Health is that state of awareness in which your intelligence, and all the elements and forces that structure your body, are in complete harmony with the elements and the forces that structure the body of the universe. When one is in complete alignment with the other, that is health. That might sound a bit abstract, but that phenomenon, of becoming aligned with one's surroundings, is perfectly natural. We call it 'entrainment'. Entrainment is a state in which there is a harmonious interaction of elements and forces between different relationships.

Can you give me an example of entrainment in nature?

There are many commonplace examples that demonstrate this principle. If you took the pendulums of five different clocks, and started them swinging at five different times, in a couple of hours you would find entrainment—they will all be swinging together. If women live together, then after a while their menstrual cycles begin to synchronise. If a mother holds her baby to her breast, after a while the baby's heartbeat begins to have a rhythmic relationship with the mother's heartbeat. You have all seen in flight a flock of birds that seem to turn at exactly the same time. Schools of fish behave in the same way. What is happening? There is certainly no time for a leader to demonstrate the direction in which they are to go. No, it happens simultaneously. This is entrainment.

When we meditate together, our breathing begins to conform to the same rhythm. And, if someone were to examine our brainwaves with an oscilloscope, the brainwaves would all conform to one pattern. All the rhythms that we know of in the body are an expression of universal rhythms. Some of these are known to science. For example, your body has a circadian rhythm, which is a result of the Earth spinning on its own axis. For every change in nature during the 24-hour cycle, there is a change that happens in you, because you are part of nature. The effect on all animals is so powerful that two identical doses of radiation given to an animal at two different times during that cycle may, on the one occasion, have hardly any effect, and, on the other, have a disastrous effect. This is because the body changes during this cycle. It changes at all levels: physically, structurally, and quantum mechanically.

That is entrainment. There are millions of examples. It is a natural phenomenon. Nature is one big mind, orchestrating the diversity of the universe. When we step out of it, then we feel discomfort, because the intelligence orchestrating it meets resistance in our body.

How do we know whether we are entrained, or in tune with the universe?

In the Ayurvedic tradition there are three principles in nature. Being familiar with them, and with your relationship to them, enables you to be more in tune with the universe. These three principles are: *vata,* meaning movement; *pitta,* meaning transformation, and *kapha,* indicating structure.

The first principle, *vata,* or movement, is derived from the first two elements in nature—space and air. It is characterised by freedom of movement.

The second principle, transformation, or *pitta,* is derived from fire, which is the symbol of transformation, of metabolic transformation. It is also derived from water.

The third structure, or *kapha,* is derived from earth and water.

Together, these principles are the five elements in nature—space, air, fire, water and earth. They relate to certain other principles in nature, certain other vibrations in nature, namely our five senses: sound, touch, sight, taste and smell. These are also called codes of intelligence, because they are our means of gaining awareness.

Consciousness is infinitely silent and flexible, and a field of infinite possibilities. It is spirit, and as it moves within itself, it creates vibrations, which express themselves as the codes of intelligence. These vibrations are expressed in a specific order as they are created: sound, touch, sight, taste and then smell. Then, these five codes of intelligence express themselves as the five elements—space, air, fire, water and earth.

This sounds like a radical simplification of nature. How can things in such a complex universe be reduced to these basic terms?

It's true, it sounds ancient and archaic. But look at your experience carefully. All that you experience— all that anybody experiences—is through the five senses, and the experience is nothing but the five elements in recycled form. Space is matter in its quantum mechanical form, air is matter in its gaseous form, fire is matter in its metabolic expression, water is matter in its liquid expression, and earth is matter in its solid expression. They are all part of a continuum of consciousness as it moves within itself, and as it changes from one into many.

But how do these things relate to my body?

We are each localised bundles of consciousness. If the space and air elements dominate in a certain localised bundle of consciousness, and, correspondingly, certain codes of intelligence dominate our consciousness, then that gives rise to certain psychophysiological tendencies. These are tendencies in the way we think and behave as well as tendencies in our body, in the expression of our body. Each person is dominated by one of the three codes, or by a mixture of two codes. If the code that dominates our awareness is sound and touch, then that physiology is called 'vata'. Vata tendencies express themselves in a certain type of appearance. Vata people are usually thin, and energetic. They can't gain weight. They are ectomorphic; that is, you can see their bones, they are lanky, and you can see the tendons and veins. Another characteristic is that their skin is usually dry—space and air. They are very mobile, both physically and mentally. They think fast, they move fast: we call them hyper-metabolic. Usually, they are vivacious, friendly, and enthusiastic. But if they are under stress these very same tendencies make them anxious, restless and unreliable. Under stress, they will develop migraine headaches, palpitations, irritable bowel syndrome, insomnia or muscle spasms, cold intolerance or weight loss. So you see how there is a positive side and a negative side: under stress there is a different, but related, set of tendencies. It is one tendency manifesting in different ways.

What do you think causes stress?

Stress is anything that blocks the intelligence. Anything that causes resistance to the flow of intelligence.

What is intelligence?

You are intelligence. Intelligence is information that knows that it is information. You have the ability to self-refer. You are conscious of your consciousness, and anything that has intelligence is capable of evolution. When information becomes alive, it is intelligence. But I have to emphasise, again, that it is non-local, everywhere. We have localised ourselves through the body, and now we often mistake ourselves for the body. William Blake wrote:

> We are led to believe a lie
> When we see with and not through the eye
> That was born in the night to perish in the night
> While the soul slept in beams of light.

Rumi, who was a Sufi poet, said it very eloquently: 'You are the unconditioned spirit that is trapped in conditions, the boundless spirit that is trapped in boundaries, like the sun and an eclipse.'

You've mentioned the characteristics of vata *people, but what about the other two body types?*

The second category of psychophysiological tendencies is *pitta,* the expression of fire and water. What are the characteristics of *pitta? Pitta* types are what we call mesomorphs. This means that their body type is more muscular and athletic. Their mental attributes are precision, discipline, order and passion. Under stress, these characteristics show up as anger, impatience, hostility, and inflammatory emotions. Fire is the ruling element, so their physical ailments will include fiery, inflamed skin such as rashes and pimples. They will get ulcers, hypertension, and inflammatory forms of arthritis such as rheumatoid arthritis. They will be prone to coronary disease. But, when they are healthy, they show courage, vitality, fearlessness, discipline and passion, and they are very articulate.

The last category is *kapha*—earth and water. Earth is solid and cool, and water is moist, so the *kapha* type will have skin that is moist and cool. They are endomorphic. If you are a *kapha,* you will gain weight just by looking at food! This is because you are hypo-metabolic. *Kapha* types are very loving, very compassionate, and they have a wonderful sense of humour. Under stress, they begin to hold onto things. Physically, they hold onto fat and fluid, but they also hold onto relationships, and become jealous and possessive. They hoard everything, including money. The physical manifestations are congestion, such as bronchial congestion; fluid retention; obesity; type 2 diabetes; and arthritis of the fluid type that is caused by fluid retention in the joints.

Can you give me more information concerning health?

I'm sure you know that there are many studies that look at the risk factors for sudden death from cardiovascular trouble. But did you know that statistics indicate that more than half of all people who die prematurely from these events did not have any of the known risk factors such as high cholesterol, and did not smoke?

Interestingly, the best predictor of a fatal coronary event is job dissatisfaction. This implies that purpose in life, what is also called the law of dharma, is vital to health. One of its components, to deal with it only briefly, is to express our unique talents.

The second-best predictor is the self-happiness rating. So happiness, or the lack of it, is a huge factor in our own mortality.

Another stunning fact is this: in our culture, more people die at nine o'clock on a Monday morning than at any other time. Ideas are harbingers of death and war. In Australia, Aborigines have a practice called 'pointing the bone', which is like a curse. People die from having the bone pointed at them. There are thousands of similar examples which show the immense power of an idea. You hear the expression 'That's just an idea.'

This is a contradiction in terms, because people don't understand how powerful ideas are, or how ideas rule their lives. But perhaps ideas could be the harbingers of peace and health as well.

What about time? Does the way we perceive time affect our health?

Time is dependent upon our perceptions. There has never been an experiment to show, or a mathematical formulation to describe, the existence of the flow of linear time. The experience of the flow of linear time is a phenomenon created by the nervous system. In fact, the past, present and future all co-exist in a field of infinite possibilities. The experience of linear time is just nature's way of preventing us from experiencing everything at once, which is how it is really happening.

You know from your own experience that when we are enjoying ourselves, time flies. When we are bored or unhappy, it crawls. Some people seem to be constantly running out of time. They see the same clocks that you or I see, but somehow these clocks seem to move much faster for them. They have speeded up their biological clocks, which gives them faster heart rates, and adrenaline is coursing through their bodies. They have all these scared platelets! When they drop dead of a heart attack, they have finally really 'run out of time'.

But just as we can access the gap between our thoughts to change our experiences, we can change the experience of time. Perhaps you have had such an experience: you may have been watching the beauty of a sunset, praying, or making love, when suddenly you slipped out of time-bound consciousness. The expression is 'time stood still'. It is when the observer and the observed become one: it is an experience of unity.

The American psychologist Abraham Maslow called it a peak experience. It is also the experience of love: love not as a mere sentiment, but as the ultimate truth at the heart of creation.

What about ageing? Do our ideas influence that, too?

There are fascinating studies which show us that ageing is not a fixed phenomenon. Really, we all know it isn't. We all know people who seem 'old before their time', or sprightly older people who seem to defy the ravages of time. But strictly controlled studies have demonstrated this very clearly. One of the most interesting studies was done at Harvard by Ellen Langer, a psychologist. In the mid-1980s, she advertised in a Boston newspaper for people over the age of seventy-five to participate in an experiment. These people were taken to a retreat where the environment was created to replicate that in 1959. The furniture was from this time, they watched movies from that period, and even the news from that period was provided. The reading material provided was from 1959—there were *Life* magazines, and so on. So all the sensory stimuli replicated those in the 1950s.

The hypothesis was that the same sensory stimulation might create the same flux of neurotransmitters and hormones as the original experience. This was based on the simple observation that we do get physical responses from imagination: if you imagine that you are eating a lemon, you'll get a flow of saliva in your mouth. And have you ever recalled an embarrassing or stressful past experience? If so, you will know that you get a surge of adrenaline through your system, or that you feel your heart pounding faster. The results in this experiment were remarkable. Within a week, several of the biomarkers that were studied had reversed. I mean the *actual* symptoms of ageing were reversed. People regained flexibility in their fingers, had improved eyesight, and so on. Because they were younger in 1959, and they were receiving the same mental information that they had at that time, their bodies responded accordingly. This leads us to an amazing conclusion: that what we know as chronological age can be reversed.

I am interested in how mind-body medicine came about. Can you comment on Western medicine and how it works, and also what its flaws are?

When I went first started medical school, I wanted to know the meaning of life. But do you know what my first experience was? I was introduced to a corpse. That is the model of Western medicine: that the body is just an anatomical structure. We think that biochemistry creates thoughts, and that, if we understand how biochemistry works, then we'll be able to solve health problems.

Modern medicine is based on the materialistic model that attempts to discover the mechanisms of disease in the hope that if you do, and you can interfere with these mechanisms, then you can get rid of disease. Now, this model is very successful. If you understand how bacteria multiply and you can find the right antibiotic, then you should be able to stop infections. Likewise, if you understand how cancer cells replicate, and you can stop this from happening, then you can get rid of cancer.

The materialistic model is very effective in the treatment of illness, in individual cases. But it is important to look at it from a more holistic viewpoint. When you consider the overall picture, we find that modern medicine does not really significantly alter overall morbidity or mortality. We know several facts that illustrate this. For example, antibiotic-resistant infections, acquired only in hospitals, are a huge problem, and that problem is growing. We also know that the Number One

...ause of addiction in the world is not street drugs but legal medical prescriptions, and that cancer is on the increase, in spite of all the money and research we throw at it.

So it is clear that the materialistic model has problems with its assumption that the mechanics of disease are also the origins of disease, not to mention the fact that it tells us nothing about the origins of health.

If you want to understand the origins of health you have to ask a deeper question. You have to ask what life is, and this is what we have been talking about. So we need to go beyond the materialistic model. About fifteen or twenty years ago many doctors saw that preventing illness was possibly much more effective than trying to cure it, and that was the start of preventative medicine. The mind-body revolution in health began when some of us saw that it was possible to evoke the healing response from within the human body itself.

Could you explain how the human body heals itself?

Your body is its own pharmacy: it makes all kinds of drugs—sleeping aids, tranquillisers, immuno-modulators. Just about any drug you can name, the body makes by itself. Not only that, but it provides the right drug at the right time, in the right dose, for the right organs. There are no side effects and all the instructions come with the packaging. That is a fact, and one that is well documented by science.

Unless our body makes a drug, our brains probably don't have the appropriate receptors for it, so in order for a drug to work it must replicate our natural pharmacy in some way. And this pharmacy is patrolled by our five senses; that is, our codes of intelligence.

Can you give a specific example of how this works?

Let's look at sound, which is the first impulse of consciousness. Our first experience of the world is through sound, and in the Ayurvedic tradition we call this first sound 'primordial sound'. Any sound in nature that creates form or phenomenon is primordial sound. Primordial sounds are basic in nature, our brains included. Our brains are made up of the same things that make up everything else (plants, stars, the bodies of other animals): they are made up of the elements earth, water, fire, space and air. Now, if you reduce all these to their essential state, you get vibrations.

Language is an evolutionary development of primordial sound. The first glimmer of consciousness in an unborn child is sound, because the first thing that develops in the infant's body is the acoustic apparatus. We first experience the world through sound, and even ancient people have known this.

There have been many recent studies on the effects of reading to children in the womb, and at the Sharp Institute [in San Diego, California] we are studying the effect of sounds on babies, because we feel that the types of sounds that a baby hears might influence its personality development. For instance, if there is a stressful environment, with the sound of hostility, and the mother is releasing stress hormones at the same time, then the baby will learn to associate the sounds with the stress.

You will find many references to sound in the ancient teachings of the world

How do you use sound for healing?

There are many ways to use sound, but each of these techniques has one goal: to bring about the process of entrainment.

One way to heal your body through sound is by learning how to localise non-local sounds. You make the sound of a vowel or a consonant, then you localise the sound, directing it to the part of your body that you want to be healed. But it is a good idea to listen to a tape of these sounds, or to attend a seminar, so that you hear them and know what sounds to make. Although making the sounds is a very powerful healing technique, it takes some time to learn how to move the sound around your body.

Can you give an example of sounds that are specifically active in particular areas in the body?

Yes. For instance, the sound 'ma' localises to the sinuses, and the sound of 'na' goes to the inner ear, so it is good for dizziness and balance. There are many others, but I don't want to give them all here. Just understand that every sound you make creates and responds to a vibration in your body. Once you become proficient at directing these sounds, you'll be able to start the healing process.

I understand that we can use these sounds to help in our own healing. What about healing others? Can you direct those sounds to someone else's sick body?

Yes, this is possible. But you need to start this process in a state of health yourself. Heal yourself first and become balanced. Then you can worry about other people.

Are these all the healing sounds? What about music and chanting?

There are many other sounds: there is a whole universe of sounds! You can create harmonic sounds by rounding out your mouth in a certain way. We also use Vedic musical sounds, recognised thousands of years ago to pertain to the different body types. For instance, if you have a *vata* problem, you play the *vata* balancing sound.

Vedic music is used for healing and it does work.

At the Sharp Institute, we have done studies on this, and so have other people. Vedic music can balance your biological rhythms, and cause the secretion of endogenous opiates, which are healing chemicals, in your body.

Chanting is a healing method that has been known for centuries, and it is practised in many different cultures. I like the word *enchantment,* which is the magic that happens with chanting. Gregorian chanting is one of the most powerful forms of chanting. There is also chanting in the Sufi tradition. They are all very powerful.

What's a mantra, then, and how can it be used?

Mantras are primordial sounds as well. The word *mantra* is from the Sanskrit meaning instrument of thought. Mantras have physiological effects and cause the release of healing chemicals in your body. One mantra is the om (*aum*), which means one, to become one with God and with the universal mind. There are mantras for healing, for bringing about change in the body. There are even mantras for bringing about a change in the environment. And of course the most important mantras are those that you use for your own spiritual discovery.

There are also sounds in nature—wind chimes, rushing streams, ocean tides—which reflect the inherent rhythms of nature. In every healing tradition in the world you will find that sound is primary in healing. Of course, it is only one of many healing techniques: besides sound there is massage, or some sort of healing using the power of touch; another is diet, or nutrition; a fourth uses herbal science; a fifth is prayer or meditation; and finally there is exercise, or some sort of healing based on movement.

You mentioned that massage is one of the universal healing techniques. How does touch help to heal?

There has been a considerable amount of research lately into the effects of touch. One discovery is that the neuropeptides found in the brain are found in the skin as well. There have also been numerous studies on the beneficial effects of the caring touch. One study, published in 1980 in *Science,* recounted research into the effects of a diet high in cholesterol. One group of rabbits, despite the diet, did not show the same high cholesterol readings, but the researchers didn't know why. They finally discovered that the technician who tended this particular group was not just feeding them, but petting and cuddling each one. Another study performed at the University of Miami revealed that premature babies who were regularly stroked gained forty-nine per cent more weight per day. Stroking the baby caused the secretion of growth hormones, or anabolic hormones. Because growth hormones in small doses also help to reverse ageing, when you massage someone you can lower their biological age. You can, it has been shown, cause the secretion of VIP— vaso-active intestinal polypeptide—when you massage someone. VIP is one of the most powerful vasal dilators known to medical science, and can increase the blood flow to the heart, which means that massage is really a very powerful tool in treating cardiovascular problems. In the Ayurvedic tradition, a daily massage is recommended.

That would be great, of course. But how many people have a personal masseur or even a partner willing to do that?

That is why we always teach people how to massage themselves! But again, the caring touch is important, so I always encourage it, too. Even just a relaxing foot massage at night can help. Our culture is not a 'touching' culture. A famous psychologist did a survey of the number of 'touch contacts' between people in an hour in different cultures. In Latin American cultures, he found that people touched one another around 170 to 180 times per hour, and in France, about ninety times per hour. But in the United States, it was only two times an hour. This illustrates what a big difference there is between cultures, and how isolated people can get in Western, Anglo-Saxon cultures.

It is easy to see how massage would be beneficial, because it makes you feel so good. What about the eyes, though? Is the sense of sight also useful in healing?

You've heard the saying 'The eyes are the windows to the soul'? Well, in yogic terms, this is very true. Your eye movements reflect what is happening in your consciousness. There are movements of the body and of the eyes which have a direct effect on consciousness, and they are known as *'mudras'*. Consciousness influences body language: you can often tell what someone is thinking by their body language. The opposite is also true: your body language influences your consciousness. There is a whole science of *mudras*. The *mudras* can create brainwave coherence.

What is brainwave coherence?

There are two fascinating and recently discovered phenomena: brainwave coherence and heart-wave coherence. Brainwave coherence is measured by an electroencephalograph, and is defined as the constancy of the relationship of brainwaves at a specified frequency when measured from different parts of the scalp. Increased brainwave coherence correlates directly with increased creativity, better memory retrieval, better attention span, and better learning ability.

Heart-wave coherence is measured by an electrocardiogram in conjunction with an instrument-based test called a 'Fourier analysis', which can analyse every part of the electrocardiogram's output. It is still being investigated, but the early results seem to suggest that traits such as aggressiveness and hostility correlate with low heart-wave coherence, and may correlate again with cardiovascular problems. The two—heart-wave coherence and brainwave coherence—can then be measured in relation to each other, and you can come up with a measure of total-body electromagnetic coherence.

Is it possible to increase heart- and brainwave coherence?

You can do it through the eye *mudras,* and through meditation, especially primordial sound meditation. The *mudras* will create a pattern of coherence in your brainwave pattern. Different *mudras* can also affect the retrieval of memory: visual, auditory, kinesthetic, emotional, olfactory, and gustatory. You can develop your third eye, too—the eye that sees past, present and future simultaneously. These *mudras* are taught in our workshops, and on some of my videos. They are simple to learn, easy to practise, and very effective, increasing creativity and enhancing health.

We also teach the heart sutra, which increases heart-wave coherence. There are eye exercises you can do that improve your eyes to make them healthier. They are also very simple techniques.

CHAPTER 4 | *The Science of Life*

All answers so far in this book have fed back into to a very exciting and dynamic part of Deepak's teachings—Ayurvedic medicine. As is widely known, most of Deepak's work in holistic health is based on Ayurveda.

Over the years, I've received countless letters from *Planet* readers regarding Ayurveda, and in response to these letters have published articles on an array of subjects, drawing upon Deepak's extensive Ayurvedic knowledge.

All this sparked my own interest in Ayurveda, and encouraged me to embark on my own Ayurvedic adventure. As part of this adventure I co-wrote a book with Karen Downes and Judith White: *Aromatherapy, Meditation and Contemplation*. I dedicated a significant portion of this book to a discussion on the relationship between aromatherapy and Ayurveda. This whetted my appetite and

I was determined to find out more about this exciting subject.

As so often happens when you focus your interest in a certain direction, answers began to come. Fortunately, they came from the insightful knowledge of Dr Vasant Lad whom many people regard as one of the leading authorities on Ayurvedic medicine. He is Director of the Ayurvedic Institute in Albuquerque. I was given a unique opportunity to speak with him during a Training in Mind/Body Medicine course in Atlanta, Georgia. Here, Dr Lad and other notable Ayurvedic doctors shared information on Ayurveda. To begin this chapter, then, I'd like to share with you what I learnt during this course. It forms a good basis for a general understanding of the subject, leading up to some more detailed answers from Deepak later in the chapter.

An Introduction to Ayurveda

What is Ayurveda?

Ayurveda is usually referred to as India's traditional medicine. It was developed by Rishis, the great masters and seers of ancient India, and forms the cornerstone of all modern Indo-European thought and language.

Ayurveda translates as 'science of life'. *Ayus* is 'life' and *veda* is 'science' or 'knowledge'. This translation certainly encompasses the fundamental basis of Ayurvedic medicine which embraces holistic healing. Ayurveda asks, 'Who is my patient?' rather than, 'What's wrong with my patient?' It therefore observes total health, including physical, emotional, mental, environmental and spiritual health.

While traditional Ayurvedic medicine takes a total approach to the human being, it doesn't necessarily focus solely on healing—prevention and maintenance of health are considered just as important.

According to Ayurveda the body and the whole universe are made up of *prana*. This literally translates as energy. In China it's called *chi* and in Japan it's referred to as *ki*. This vital energy reveals itself as earth, water, fire, air and ether. When these elements are unbalanced in the body, disease or illness is given the chance to manifest. Energy of the body has to be kept in balance through the use of other energies that come in the form of breath, food, water, sunshine, exercise, and sleep. Now, energy in these forms isn't going to be the same for everyone: they must be used in co-operation with the unique characteristics of the individual.

So Ayurvedic medicine focuses on the individual. It recognises that each of us is unique and as such should be treated according to our own needs.

But doesn't Ayurveda divide all people into three body types? Surely this isn't very liberating if we're limited to only one of three sub-categories.

True, Ayurveda does speak specifically of three separate body types or *doshas,* and I'll discuss these in greater detail in a moment. Yet this doesn't mean that a person is restricted to only one body type. Although one or two may dominate, most of us are a combination of all three.

While it's important to find out your body type (by determining the type that dominates), it's even more important to determine how you react to certain foods, environments, emotions, and so on. The onus is on the individual to get more in tune with themselves.

The body type provides a guide, yet Ayurveda is essentially about discovering who you are holistically, then encouraging you to be the very best you can be.

Please don't think the body type definitions define the limits of your potential. A correct understanding of your body type will simply give you access to your genuine nature and to your healthy, beautiful, perfectly balanced self.

Can you briefly summarise the whole idea of body types?

According to Ayurveda, the life energy or *prana* is channelled through our bodies by the 'wind' known as *vata*. *Vata* is one of three metabolic principles (*doshas*) that give form to every living thing. (*Vata* is air and space.) The other two *doshas* are *pitta* and *kapha*. *Pitta* is fire and water, and *kapha*, earth and water.

A small number of people are purely *vata*, *pitta* or *kapha*, while most people are a combination of two or three. Each of the three *doshas* has certain basic, well-defined functions.

Vata types usually have a thin, light build, and, while they can perform activities quickly, they tire easily. Their hunger and digestion may be irregular and their sleep is often light and interrupted.

They are usually enthusiastic, vivacious and imaginative, and their emotions can change quickly and under stress may be transformed into anxiety. (Impulsive eating is also evident when they are under stress.) When seriously unbalanced, *vatas* use calories as nervous energy rather than storing them as fat.

In general, *vata* people are unpredictable. *Vata* goes out of balance more quickly than the other *doshas,* so it's important for them to nurture stability and regularity of habits.

Pitta people are usually of medium build, with average levels of strength and endurance. They are fair in appearance with ruddy, often freckled, skin. They feel hunger and thirst acutely, have strong digestive systems and hate to skip meals.

They are often sharp-witted, bold, outspoken, argumentative and jealous. When in balance they are warm and ardent in their emotions. *Pitta* types often over-eat, spurring stomach and intestinal pain and heartburn. The good news is that *pitta* people are not short of self-discipline and therefore find losing weight and sticking to an exercise program easy.

Kapha people are of solid build, with great physical endurance and strength. They move slowly and gracefully, their skin is cold, smooth and pale, their digestion is slow and their hunger mild.

Kaphas tend to be relaxed and tranquil, are heavy sleepers and are prone to obesity. They are usually affectionate, tolerant and forgiving, but under stress can become complacent and possessive. *Kaphas* usually enjoy sound health, but because they seek comfort in food, they often struggle throughout their lives with weight.

Kaphas must face the fact that their body does not conform to the media's ideal of a hyper-thin build and that this in no way implies a lack of beauty. Because their digestion and metabolism are inherently slow, they tend to lose weight gradually. Once *kapha* types achieve a balance they will naturally return to their ideal weight.

How does Ayurveda explain hunger?

Ayurveda says that hunger comes from the digestive fires known as *agnis*. (*Agni* literally means 'fire'.) Ayurveda describes the process of digestion in terms of heat, as if the food is actually being burned before it is further processed. When you're hungry the *agni* is burning hotter. It is our *agni,* or our digestive capacity, that allows us to assimilate properly the foods we eat and to convert them into energy rather than fat and toxins.

Ayurveda describes a product of improper digestion as *ama*. *Ama* is both an abstract principle and a material element. Materially it is a white, sticky substance that clogs all the normal channels of flow in the physiology. These channels are not only for the passage of blood and lymph, but for normal energy. Because it blocks the channels of circulation in the physiology, *ama* is an extremely common precursor to a wide variety of diseases, and it causes the symptoms so common in overweight people: lethargy, dullness, erratic eating habits, compulsive eating, distortion of hunger sensations, and obesity itself.

You can literally see *ama*. How many times have you noticed a white coating on your tongue, especially after you've awakened? This is *ama*, and if it is present on your tongue, it is present throughout your physiology.

But *ama* has a positive counterpart that can also be present throughout the body. By eating properly and following the correct routines, this different and opposite product of digestion, called *ojas*, can be formed. Ayurveda describes *ojas* as the biochemical equivalent of bliss. By creating *ojas* within your physiology you are literally storing up the physical manifestation of joy and total well-being.

When you take steps to eliminate *ama*, more *ojas* is automatically produced. Likewise, by taking steps to enhance *ojas*, you will create less *ama*. So it is useful to know the symptoms of both these important substances. After eating a particular meal, if you feel the symptoms relating to *ama*, then you know that something was wrong with the food [as far as your particular physiology is concerned]. But if you felt the symptoms of *ojas*, you know that your physiology is being nourished and balanced by it.

Evidence of *ama* includes weakness, heaviness, lethargy, poor immunity, irregular elimination, fatigue, and fluctuations in appetite, energy levels and moods. Also, as mentioned, there is commonly a white coating on the tongue, especially in the morning.

Evidence of *ojas* includes lightness of body, excellent energy, strong appetite and digestion, perfect immunity, regular elimination, physical strength and stamina, and a general bliss. Both physically and mentally, there is an experience of vitality and intense well-being.

Are there certain tips each different body type should take into consideration?

Certainly. *Vata* types should take meals on a regular basis and be sure to select a balanced variety of foods. They should avoid cold food and drink which will immediately unbalance the *dosha*. Emphasis is on heavy, hearty foods like stews, breads and warm desserts that have a settling and comforting effect. *Vatas* should thoroughly cook almost everything so that it is easier to digest, and raw fruits and vegetables should make up only a small part of a *vata's* diet.

Pitta types should eat moderately, avoid eating when angry or emotional and try to take meals in relaxed settings. Eating outdoors amongst the beauty of nature is especially good. *Pittas* benefit from cold drinks and salads and should avoid spicy or very hot food and keep meat a relatively small part of the diet. *Pittas* are well suited to a vegetarian diet, thriving on fresh, unprocessed foods.

Kapha types should avoid ice-cream, butter, milk, rich desserts and other high-fat and sweet foods, including anything fried or oily. They would do best choosing light, warm food instead. Most importantly, *kaphas* should eat only when hungry, rather than at specified mealtimes, and will often benefit from fasting one day a week on fruit juice or skim milk which can result in greater energy and alertness.

What else constitutes an Ayurvedic treatment?

Once an individual has determined their main body type, they should then determine the best ways in which to bring themselves back into balance, not just by dietary changes but through exercise, yoga, meditation, massage, herbal tonics, herbal sweat baths, medicated enemas, and medicated inhalations. The best way to determine this is to visit an Ayurvedic practitioner.

Finally, can you give me a few tips on what exercises will suit each different body type?

Kapha types require the most exercise, *vatas* the least and *pittas* somewhere in between. If you are a two-*dosha* type, let your overall physical structure be your guide. If you're large, muscular, athletic, and *kapha* is one of your dominant *doshas*, then

THE SCIENCE OF LIFE | 79

put yourself in the *kapha* category. If you're muscular and your physical development is mixed, put yourself in the *vata* category. Those in-between should consider themselves in the *pitta* category.

Vata types will find yoga, dance, aerobics, short hikes and light cycling the most suitable forms of exercise. *Vata* types should be cautious, however, because too much exercise can throw *vata* out of balance.

Activities suited to *pitta* types are more vigorous, including skiing, walking or running, hiking, mountain climbing and swimming. For *kapha* types, running, weight training, aerobics, rowing and dance are appropriate forms of exercise.

These are just a few examples for each *dosha*, but you shouldn't feel restricted to them. Above everything else, you should participate in an exercise routine you enjoy.

When you force yourself to enjoy exercise, you release stress hormones such as adrenaline and noradrenaline, which may have an adverse effect on the immune system and other parts of the body. Also, if you dislike any particular form of exercise, your body will resist it and serious injury might result. On the other hand, if you enjoy a particular workout, your physiology will reflect that state of mind. Playing with your children or mucking around with the dog can often be more beneficial than a vigorous exercise program that you don't enjoy.

If you don't get pleasure from exercise of any kind, it may be because you have a *kapha* imbalance. As you regulate your *kapha dosha* and bring it back into balance, you'll realise that everyone enjoys some sort of exercise, and that excessive *kapha* was responsible for making you feel dull and lethargic.

Deepak discusses this fascinating subject in a little more detail.

What are the practical benefits of understanding body types?

As you become aware of yourself and your tendencies, you also become more aware of cycles and rhythms in nature. As the Earth moves and creates the circadian rhythms, there are cycles in nature that correspond to these principles. These periods occur every day and knowing them can help you function more effectively.

From 6am to 10am is a *kapha* period [for everyone]. If you are *kapha*, your body is slowing down at this time. If you are *vata*, then you slow down too, but not as much. This is the best time for vigorous exercise. From 10am to 2pm is *pitta* time, a transformation time. The sun is in its zenith, so fire—*pitta*—is dominant in the body. Because the digestive fire is strongest now, this is the time when we all get maximum benefit from nutrition. Ayurveda says that you should take your main meal of the day at noon, not at night, as is our habit in Western cultures.

From 2pm to 6pm is a *vata* phase. This is a time of activity. If you're engaged in creative activity, this is the time of maximum mental efficiency. From 6pm to 10pm is the second *kapha* phase. Now, your body starts to slow down, reaching its slowest point at 10pm. So, naturally, this is the time to wind down from the day's activities. This is the time to read a book, relax, watch a movie, to take a walk, or to look at the moon and stars. If you go to bed by 10 or 10.30pm, your sleep will be most restful because you are having it at the nadir point.

From 10pm to 2am is the second *pitta* phase. Again, the metabolic fire begins to work. This time it works to renew your body and to rid it of toxins. But if you stay awake, if you are not asleep, what happens? You raid the refrigerator. From 2am to 6am is the second *vata* phase. It manifests in rapid eye movement and dreams. In the Ayurvedic tradition, this is the time to clear mental toxicity and stress through dreams. Dreams are very good for stress release. This is a period of slow awakening. If you wake up around the end of this period, you will have maximum energy for the rest of the day.

Do these three principles relate at all to the seasons?

Yes, they do. The circadian rhythm is just the first biological rhythm. The second occurs as the Earth orbits around the sun. We go around the sun, too! Just as there are cycles or seasons in the universe, there are cycles or seasons in the body. Our body changes in so many ways: biologically, hormonally, biochemically, structurally, quantum mechanically and emotionally.

You might have guessed that summer is *pitta*. If you are a *pitta* kind of person, then during summer you will have pitta problems. It is a time for a *pitta* person to be very careful. Winter, which is cold and moist, is *kapha*. Autumn, which is a time for change, is *vata*. The early spring is *kapha,* and the late spring is *pitta*. If you were to follow an Ayurvedic program, you would make minor changes in your diet over the seasons depending on your body type. In fact, many people do that naturally. Different foods appeal to us in different seasons if we are tuned into nature.

There is another cycle in nature. As the Earth, moon and sun move in relationship to each other they create another cycle, the 28-day lunar cycle. The menstrual cycle is a 28-day lunar cycle. During the lunar cycle, prolactin (a hormone secreted by the pituitary gland) levels change, as do levels of melatonin (another hormone, secreted by the pineal gland).

And this lunar cycle also relates to the three body types?

Yes. A full moon is a *kapha* period. No moon or a new moon is a *vata* period. In between is a *pitta* period. Everyone has heard full moon stories. Well, when people do strange things at full moon, it is *kapha* types getting aggravated—maybe becoming possessive or jealous. Conversely, the complete absence of the moon will aggravate *vata* tendencies.

There is yet another rhythm or cycle in nature. As the Earth is influenced by the gravitational effect of the sun and the moon, you have another rhythm: the rhythm of the ocean tides.

Shakespeare wrote: 'There is a tide in the affairs of men.' This is literally true. We have an ocean inside of us. This ocean has the same constituents as the ocean outside. In fact, we came out of that ocean. We were once all in that primordial soup, and when we stepped out of it, we brought it out with us. Eighty per cent of our bodies is water. Just like the ocean, we have tidal rhythms inside of us. High tide is a *kapha* period, low tide is a *vata* period, and in between is a *pitta* period.

Are you saying that if we are entrained with all these rhythms in nature then we will be in complete harmony and therefore in complete health?

When the body is in complete health it is part of this cosmic dance. You are in complete harmony with all the elements and forces as they dance their dance through your physiology. When this happens, you feel vital, light, creative and full of life. You are alert and joyful because you are dancing to the rhythm of the universe.

We all know how nutrition affects health. Is there anything else we should know about food and its relationship with our body?

In Ayurveda the most important thing is that you eat consciously, that you witness the process of eating. By doing this you actually change the way food is metabolised in the body. You can do something called 'eating meditation', which is done in silence so it is best done alone. First, look at the food, and thank the provider, God or nature. Before you pick up a mouthful, have the intention that you are going to notice the intention to pick this food up. When you put it in your mouth, notice the intention to taste the food and to notice its texture. You notice your intention to chew the food, and to swallow it, and to experience the sensation in your stomach. Experience the awareness of all your intentions as you intend it, keeping silent all the time. If you practise this on a regular basis, you will be surprised at how aware you become of the effects of food in your body, how it causes changes in your body. Your body will start telling you which foods are best for you, and they will match the Ayurvedic nutritional principles of using *vata, pitta* and *kapha*.

How does taste relate to the body types?

Food itself can be categorised by its taste, and each body type will respond differently to these different tastes. There are six tastes: sweet, sour, salty, bitter, astringent and pungent.

Sweet is not just sugary things, but includes bread, rice, complex carbohydrates, chicken, fish and meat. Sour foods include yoghurt, cheese, vinegar and citrus. Salty tastes are immediately recognisable. Bitter tastes are less popular in Western culture, but are found in green leafy vegetables such as fenugreek, spinach and in some Ayurvedic herbs. Astringent tastes are found in legumes, and pungent tastes are found in spices— mustard, peppers, garlic, horseradish—all the spices.

Each taste is important to our diet, but the type of body you have will determine which sorts of foods are most beneficial for you. The hyper-metabolic tendencies of *vata* can be alleviated by a combination of sweet, sour, and salt. *Kapha,* which is hypo-metabolic, is stimulated by bitter, pungent and astringent tastes, while *pitta* is balanced by a combination of astringent, bitter and sweet tastes. Remember that these will also be affected by the seasons: in the season in which your particular body type ailments are aggravated, you should pay closer attention to the correct types of food. But it is all a matter of balance. You need all six tastes every day.

Are there other principles of Ayurvedic nutrition besides the types of food?

Yes. A lot of them are confirmed by all the nutritional science of our modern times. For instance, as I have already mentioned, you should eat your biggest meal at lunch, not in the evening as so many people do these days. In the evenings, before sunset preferably, you should have a light meal. Drink lots of water, eight to ten glasses per day, and if you want to get rid of toxins in your body, sip hot water all day long with a few drops of lemon or ginger. But don't drink at mealtimes and don't drink iced drinks.

Is fasting part of Ayurvedic nutrition?

Again, that depends on your body type. *Kapha* types should probably fast and only drink hot water, fruit juice and herbal teas. *Pitta* types would fast less frequently and *vata* types probably not at all. But this all relates to how healthy you are, and I wouldn't want to give blanket rules. However, short fasts are probably fine—24-hour fasts. Fasting has spiritual benefits as well.

Does Ayurveda use aromatherapy?

The smell receptors are extensions of the hypothalamus which is also called 'the brain's brain'. Since it is connected to the limbic system, a system concerned with autonomic (or automatic) functions, it is very primal and important to normal functioning. Through the hypothalamus, smell is directly involved with sex, eating, the flight-or-fight response, and other autonomic functions such as heart rate, and so on. Memory, behaviour and smell are closely linked. Mothers and babies know each other's smell, and so do lovers. Ayurveda has used its own form of aromatherapy for centuries—a long time before it became fashionable! In Ayurveda, there are three types of smell: the floral and fruity aromas, which are *vata* balancing, spicy smells which are *kapha* balancing, and cooling aromas which are *pitta* balancing. You can also use smell in neuro-associative conditioning. Do you remember I told you about the experiment with mice who learned to associate the smell of camphor with immune-boosting injections, and who eventually did not need the injections at all? We can do similar things. We can teach people to deal with a disorder by going into the gap and alleviating it, and release an appropriate aroma at the same time. Eventually, the aroma will cause the same physiological reaction.

Are there any practical guidelines regarding Ayurveda and life force, or prana?

Prana is really life-giving energy, and yes there are ways to enhance it, or to access sources of it. I recommend six daily practices to increase *prana*. The first is direct contact with the Earth itself—not through the soles of your shoes, but through your bare feet or better still, your whole body. The Earth is like a womb and you should give your attention to that. The second source is the breath of the plants. It is a scientific fact, of course, that we and plants are constantly exchanging gases with each other: Ayurveda calls it *prana*. Try to breathe in the air around lush vegetation, especially at sunset. Sunlight is another source but you should be careful not to overexpose yourself. Bathing in a natural body of water is another. The fifth source is food and the principle here is that it should be alive and fresh. Fresh fruits, vegetables and grains should be eaten. For instance, canned food is not alive. Overcooked food is not alive. The final source of *prana* is the stars. *Prana* is not separate energy, it is part of the energy of the universe, and is called different things in different cultures.

When I was first introduced to Ayurvedic medicine I knew absolutely nothing about it. But after spending a lot of time with Deepak over the years my desire to know more increased. That desire was sated when I went to Delhi to attend the wedding of Deepak's daughter, Mallika. I had the greatest time. People flew in from all over the world for one full week of festivities. It was more than a wedding; it was a gathering of Chopra friends and family under one marquee to welcome Sumant Mandal (Mallika's husband) and the whole Mandal clan.

While I was there, I was fortunate enough to connect with some of the most learned and compassionate healers in the world. Their background in the principles of Ayurvedic medicine was so extensive that the opportunity was too good to pass up. I turned on my trusty recorder and gathered as much information as I possibly could about the incredible array of products that Deepak has developed over the years.

The first formula I heard about was Biochavan. I was told that Chavan is the name of an Ayurvedic doctor, possibly mythical, who first created this formula. According to myth, several thousand years ago a great Indian Raj had been warring with a neighbouring country. In order to create harmony, an Indian King who was in his seventies married the daughter of the neighbouring ruler who was in her twenties. The King was concerned that he would not have the potency to satisfy this young woman and thus not be able to create offspring that would reunite the families. The King went to his Ayurvedic doctors and asked them to create a formula that would give him the vigour and vitality of his youth.

The modern-day Biochavan is said to be based on this formula created for the King. It is described as a rejuvenative, and its list of ingredients is long.

I found out that the most important ingredient is a fruit called *amalaki*. It is said to have the highest source of vitamin C on the planet.

One of the most exciting things I discovered was that Biochavan can slow the ageing process. I was also told that it makes people who are healthy even healthier. According to the information I gathered, this formula is even more effective when it is processed with ghee and honey, for this enables the herb to be synthesised more rapidly. Biochavan, because it is rich in antioxidants, also helps cells deal more effectively with stress.

One doctor seemed to sum Biochavan up best when he said it was like an Ayurvedic multi-vitamin.

Another area of interest were Deepak's Opti products. I was told they were developed to meet the needs of the people who visited the Chopra Center; they were a response to the more common and most specific concerns of patients.

OptiEnergy, for example, was designed for people who have chronic fatigue syndrome (CFS), a popular concern for many people these days. According to Ayurveda, this condition is due to a weakness in a person's digestive power—their *agni*. These people are unable to extract nourishment from their environment, including food, and are therefore creating toxicity in their system and not generating the energy that they need to have good mental clarity and physical endurance. OptiEnergy consists of five specific herbs which are considered to be invigorating or revitalising. I was assured that these herbs were not like caffeine, which simply stimulates—instead they provide cells with a use-able source of energy. I was told that OptiEnergy is recommended for people who are feeling exhausted most of the time, either because they have been working particularly hard and haven't had time to catch up, or they've had chronic illnesses which depleted their energy levels.

Then there are the OptiMan and OptiWoman formulas which are also considered to be rejuvenatives, or tonics. The herbs in these products are specifically designed for either a man's or a woman's physiology. In the men's formula the predominant two herbs are *kapikacchu* and *ashwagandha,* and these two classic male herbs are said to provide the dynamic, goal-oriented and powerful energy associated with men. In the women's formula the most common herb is *shitavari,* which is a form of Indian asparagus. This has been shown to normalise menstruation, and is recommended for menopausal women who are having mood swings. The Biochavan, OptiMan and OptiWoman are considered to complete the whole Ayurvedic approach to physical well-being, along with the most important considerations like meditating, having a daily routine and eating healthy foods.

The next 'opti' is OptiCalm. OptiCalm contains *vata* pacifying herbs such as *jatamomsi.* I was told that it is used when someone has so much brain activity that they simply can't think straight. These people usually find that, when it's time to go to sleep, they can't turn off the noise. Again it is recommended that OptiCalm be used in conjunction with other things to provide a balanced lifestyle. It is important to look at the underlying cause if you are not sleeping. Is it because you are drinking six cups of coffee a day? Or you're in a job you shouldn't be in? Or you're in a terrible relationship?

OptiMind is obviously for the mind. Its main herb is *brahmi*. There are about four or five different herbs in Ayurveda that have been given the name *brahmi*. The one present in OptiMind has been shown to quieten but maintain alertness in the mind. It also consists of other herbs designed to help people think more efficiently. It's good for students who are studying for exams, and for people who think their memory is fading or simply need clarity. It's also used by people who have CFS. Some people with CFS not only feel that their bodies are tired but they also have trouble with their minds. In such cases OptiEnergy and OptiMind are often recommended as a good combination.

As we continue down the list we come to OptiMetabolise which I was told helps to enhance and balance the metabolic system. According to Ayurveda, obesity is a result of incomplete digestion. Usually this happens when people are trying to fulfil an emotional need through food, or they are not recognising their body's signals and they take in more than the body can use. In Ayurveda, one of the doctors explained, OptiMetabolise is designed to do four things. One is to stimulate the digestive *agni*, the digestive fire, so that when you eat the body uses up the food completely. The second is to stimulate the tissue digestive fires, the tissue *agnis,* so that whatever you stored in the tissues you can begin to eliminate. The third is to enhance elimination so that your digestive system works and does not leave unwanted remnants of food in your body. (Ayurveda states that one or two bowel movements a day is normal, anything less than that is not.) The final thing is that it helps to cleanse the blood.

For people who have a weak appetite there is OptiDigest. I agreed with the viewpoint that one of two things can happen to people who are under a lot of emotional stress. They can eat a lot, even though they don't need the food. Or they can lose their appetite. I'm sure we all know people who say things like 'I'm just not that hungry', 'Food doesn't look that good to me' or 'I have to force myself to eat'. Cancer patients often have trouble with appetite, even though they must eat in order to build up their strength. The main herb in OptiDigest is *trikatu,* and there are some other digestive stimulants as well. *Trikatu* means 'three pungents', and is based on a classic formula. Another good formula for digestion is OptiAci Neutral, which is good for people who have a lot of excessive *pitta,* particularly in their upper digestive tract. Again it's not recommended that you keep on taking this formula for weeks at a time. You need to discover what it is your body is telling you about the underlying imbalance.

OptiAbsorb is designed for people who have irritable bowel syndrome, and it's also for people who have trouble eating, digesting and eliminating. I was told that, at any one time, thirty per cent of the population of the United States of America is complaining of some form of functional bowel problem. Western medicine, once it has ruled out ulcers, inflammatory bowel disease or colon cancer, doesn't know what to do for these people. OptiAbsorb was designed to help.

The last 'opti' is OptiElim, a formula that helps to smooth bowel movements and is recommended for people who have a tendency towards constipation, particularly *vata* types. OptiElim is said to be balancing and tonifying to the colon.

After discussing the Opti products with my esteemed company, I asked what was the purpose of Ayurvedic teas and spices. I was reminded of the Ayurvedic principle that suggests that anything you put on your tongue stimulates one of six tastes: sweet, sour, salty, bitter, pungent or astringent. Although each of us needs different proportions of these in order to feel completely satisfied, at the end of a meal we should have had a sampling of each of the six tastes. Then, based on our own mind-body constitution, we will discover which three of these tastes we favour. A simple and easy way to meet this particular principle is to use the specially designed Ayurvedic herb-and-spice blends. They remove any need to worry about a meal having each of these flavours. Instead, if you are sautéeing some vegetables or making up some pasta, you can sprinkle on the spice blend that is for your mind-body type.

The teas are similar and are made up of pure spices. So, some spices will be more stimulating, some more calming, and others cooling to your system. If you have a strong tendency towards insomnia and anxiety, and your mind is racing, then drinking a cup of *vata* tea before bedtime will help to quieten your mind. If you tend to get irritated easily and to have a temper, then drinking some *pitta* tea will help to cool you down. And finally, if you tend to have trouble starting in the morning, overeat and feel quite heavy, then taking some *kapha* tea can be very helpful.

In my discussions about these products it soon became very apparent that these formulas were not recommended for people who weren't prepared to consider the entire Ayurvedic program. While the Biochavan and OptiMan and OptiWoman might be possible exceptions, it was made very clear that the other formulas would not be helpful unless someone was interested in getting to the source of a problem.

The main point was that these formulas, teas and spices are only one aspect of a total, holistic health program. For example, it would never be recommended that someone take OptiCalm rather than learn primordial sound meditation.

Other than the Biochavan and OptiMan and OptiWoman formulas, the rest of the formulas would not be taken for more than a couple of months at a time. People who feel they still need the herbs after this time are encouraged to look deeper and find out why they are still having problems, because neither Deepak nor any of the staff at the Chopra Center for Well Being would suggest that the herbs be a substitute for greater evolution or greater overall holistic health care.

CHAPTER 5 | Quenching Your Spiritual Thirst

I've often said enlightenment is available to anyone at the snap of a finger. It's your choice if you want to sit on a hill in Tibet for five years, drinking miso and eating alfalfa sprouts and tofu while contemplating the meaning of life. But don't be fooled into believing this is the only form of enlightenment. Enlightenment comes in many different ways. It can come when you hear a couple of lines of poetry that really have an impact on you, or when listening to a song. It could happen that three words of one song change your life forever—as simple as that.

I saw part of a TV show in which the most untidy, disorganised and unconventional detective in the squad solved the case. The young constable turned to the inspector and asked, 'How do you do it? You're a walking disaster area when it comes to procedures.' The inspector answered, 'Never be frightened to walk out of step with others, because you'll walk on ground no one else touches.' I thought, 'Wow, I've been doing that all my life without even thinking about it.'

That was a little piece of instant enlightenment for me. If I'd chosen, I could have come to the same conclusion by meditating or contemplating. Instead, I came upon this small piece of enlightenment simply by flicking TV stations during commercial breaks.

From this experience I realised that quenching your spiritual thirst does not have to be an almighty quest. It can be, if you wish, simply little sips or mouthfuls along the way.

Deepak puts this in context, and gives it the depth it deserves.

What is spirituality?

Spirituality is that domain of awareness in which we experience our universality, that place where you and I connect. It's also the source of creativity and thought. Remember, we are not our thoughts. Thoughts are like guests—they check in and check out. But you are always there.

The spirit is the real you that's behind the scene, beyond the mind. It's also beyond the subconscious. It's absolutely clear, infinitely creative and infinitely flexible.

Why should we engage in spiritual seeking?

Well, if you ask a seer or a sage that question, he or she will answer 'Why not?' Is it not fascinating?

Do you ever have lapses in faith and spirituality?

Yes, I do in fact. And when I do, I take a week off and go to the desert and escape from the world. I don't have any contact with the world—no faxes, no phones, no communication, not even a television or books. And I spend a whole week in silence and I feel renewed when I do that, and I do that three or four times a year.

You've written a book called The Way of the Wizard. *I'd like to know why the wizard's way is so valuable?*

The wizard is rooted in creativity and is therefore supremely intelligent. It has a way of thinking that is not linear or rational but intuitive, wise and nourishing, and the wizard's way is not oriented to direct cause and effect. Yet, because of its computing ability, it is infinitely intelligent and far more active than anything in rational thought. Using the wizard's way will help us to recognise higher states of awareness leading ultimately to pure consciousness as a consequence.

*Earlier you mentioned the 'shadow' of the self.
How important is it that we embrace our shadow?*

It's extremely important to embrace the shadow because when we look inside ourselves we will find that we are a conglomeration of ambiguities, and an assortment of different archetypal energies that stoke the fire of life in our souls. Within all of us there is both the sacred and the profane, the divine and the diabolical, the sinner and saint, the dark light of the soul and paradise, and it is only by going through these secret passages, dark alleys and ghost-filled attics of our own mind that we can find the bliss of pure consciousness. Moreover, unless we embrace our own shadows we are likely to be extremely judgmental of others, and this moral self-righteousness and need to judge causes turbulence with our internal dialogue, which in turn causes us to lose our connection with the spirit. Therefore, embracing the shadow is a very useful technique to begin spontaneously to become non-judgmental.

*Why become non-judgmental? How is that
valuable?*

All experience is experienced in a world of meaningful contrasts: good and bad, right and wrong, dark and light, night and day. These contrasts are essential, and life moves within the poles of these opposites. When we accept this, we stop trying to control and judge. We try not to label everything right or wrong, good or bad, but realise that these are simply two sides of the same coin, both relative to the other. Ceasing from judgment is part of silencing your internal dialogue.

I once heard a beautiful prayer that goes:

Today I will judge nothing that occurs
And as I judge nothing that occurs I will create
    silence in my mind
And as I create silence in my mind I will communi-
    cate with the cosmic mind that is running and
    orchestrating the machinery of the universe
The cosmic mind whispers to us in the silent
    spaces between our thoughts.

Judgments are so debilitating because they cause turbulence in our internal dialogue and cause heaviness of the heart.

Is there anything in the universe that never changes?

The only thing that never changes is the spirit itself. Yet that's a paradox because all that appears in the field of change is also a manifestation of spirit. So there is only one thing in the universe that is simultaneously change and non-change at the same time, and that is spirit.

You have talked about spiritual laws—for instance, the law of dharma—and you have published a book called The Seven Spiritual Laws of Success. *Our culture is not used to spiritual laws. How are they relevant to us today?*

Understanding and acting on the seven spiritual laws is effective. Why? Because they are not laws handed down from an authority; they are not rules. They are really descriptions of how the universe works, how nature's intelligence operates, and how it manifests in the wonderful diversity of the world. They are like the laws of nature. You don't obey the laws of nature as such. You won't get put in jail for trying to break the laws. But you won't have any success in trying to flout them either!

The spiritual laws are simply the mechanics by which the pure soul transforms itself into matter: that which allows the unfolding from the world of the unmanifest to the world of the manifest. The spontaneous flow of intelligence, of energy and information, exists in everything that is alive. You experience success in all sorts of ways—emotional, material, physical and spiritual—when you understand the laws and bring your life into harmony with them.

Each law expresses a truth, and its practice brings us happiness.

How do you define success?

Success can be described in a number of different ways. We can describe it as 'progressively fulfilling worthwhile goals'; or we can use the criterion of fulfilment of desire, or the idea of happiness. People can become immensely wealthy and be neither happy nor healthy, so perhaps their goals were not worthwhile, and their desires were harmful. Everyone wants to be happy, but if you question people in the street, you'll find that most people, if you use this criterion, are unsuccessful.

So the relevance of the laws is clear: the laws help to create success and happiness in our lives. By practising them, you may find that your ideas of success, and the things you valued before, are changing. So don't see them as rules, or as codes of behaviours, but as explanations of how the universe works. If you stop fighting against these natural laws, you start to be more attuned to your own true nature.

Can you explain what these laws are?

The first law is the law of pure potentiality, and it states that, in my essential self, I am spirit. You can call it God, you can call it what scientists call it— the unified field—or you can call it what the physicist David Baume calls it—the 'implicit order from which everything is unfolded'. When we have the direct experience of that—not just the intellectual understanding—then we experience pure joy, perfect balance, and simplicity. When our internal reference point becomes that, we are no longer fearful of challenges, fearful of being hurt, fearful of dying, and so on.

I have to say right now that the law of pure potentiality doesn't sound like something I can practise. How do I act on such a law?

You get in touch with your essential self by going into the gap as we discussed before. You meditate, you spend time with yourself. Many of us live with a perfect stranger—our inner self. If we don't spend any time alone with ourselves, how are we going to know ourselves? When we want to know the totality of everything, we have to know the mind. So we practise silence, we commune with nature, and we practise non-judgment.

The second law is that of giving. That rests on the idea of dynamic exchange, on the idea that giving and receiving are just different aspects of the flow of energy through the universe. When we give that which we seek, we keep the abundance of the universe circulating through our lives.

What happens when we stop giving?

The opposite happens: we stop the flow. We interfere with the natural flow. You have to keep giving; otherwise you decay. It is important to give willingly, joyfully, because when we do that the giving becomes its own good, its own joy, its own emotional fulfilment, and the other rewards—physical, material rewards—follow. You should think: 'Whoever I encounter, I will give them a gift, and I will also receive gratefully anything anyone has to offer. I make a commitment to keep wealth circulating in my life, and in order to do so I will keep giving away the most precious things in life.'

What are the most precious things in life?

The most essential human needs, according to psychologists, are affection, attention, appreciation and love, and, although this seems obvious when you think about it, our culture doesn't recognise it. Remember that survey of touching that I told you about? If we started to touch each other lovingly, we would probably do more good for our overall health status than we would with any other measure. Listening is important too: listen with the totality of your being. Notice and appreciate the qualities and giving of others. These gifts cost nothing, but you start the process. You can also activate the law of pure potentiality by receiving gifts with gratitude.

The third spiritual law is the law of karma, and we have talked about karma as meaning action. At every moment you are faced with an infinity of choices, but there is only one choice that is karmically appropriate. That choice will bring joy to us and to anyone else affected by that choice.

How do we know which choice is the appropriate one?

The best way is consciously to witness the choices we are making as we make them. There is no need to define or judge it; just witness it. As you do, you bring it from the unconscious realm to the conscious, and you can foresee the consequences of this choice. Ask yourself what the choice will bring, not only to you but to anyone else affected. And ask your *heart* for guidance rather than your brain. Your heart gives you clear messages of comfort and discomfort, at the finest level of feeling, so you will know the right choice. Your body will tell you whether it is right or wrong.

This brings me to the fourth spiritual law. The fourth law is the law of least effort. This law goes against everything our culture has taught us. In nature, there is the principle of economy of effort. Flowers are not trying to grow, birds are not trying to fly ... In other words, nature doesn't work hard. We do, because we are out of tune with the workings of nature. We think we have to work hard to be successful. We think we have to control everything. We are like the man on the train who insists on carrying his burden on his shoulders when there is no need—the train will take him and his load to where he is going. Like him, we can set down our burdens, and life will not stop.

Doesn't hard work bring material success, at least?

Yes, but at what cost? You get this limited success, and you get heart attacks, you get divorced, your friendships suffer, you drink too much. The natural way is to 'do less, accomplish more', and ultimately, to do nothing and accomplish everything.

How do I start cultivating this effortlessness in my own life?

There are three principles that will start the process: acceptance of this moment, responsibility and defencelessness. Acceptance means to accept your situation in this moment just as it is. You accept that this moment is as it should be, that it is the result of everything else that has happened and is happening. If I struggle against this moment then I struggle against everything.

What if things are not going as you want them to go?

Then you let go of your idea of how things ought to be. We want things to go according to our plans, but our plans are not always appropriate.

Recognise that your plans and ideas may not take everything into account.

Responsibility, the second principle that will bring about the right choice, means being able to have creative responses to every situation, as we have discussed. It also rests on not blaming anyone else—for example, your parents—who may have abused you as a child. Responsibility also means surrendering to the pain as well as the pleasure.

The final principle for making the appropriate choice is defencelessness, which means a complete and total relinquishing of the need to defend your point of view. When you think of it, most of the conflict in the world rests on defending a point of view. Wars are the ultimate defence of a point of view.

How does it help to stop defending your point of view?

The need to defend a point of view is an ego-based need. When you change your internal reference point, and shift it away from the ego, then you don't need to defend the fear-driven ego. And when you do that, you become invincible, because there is nothing left to attack. How can anyone hurt me if I know that what is truly my self is beyond space and time? If you are beyond that which is born and dies, then there is no question whatsoever of defence, or of being hurt.

The fifth spiritual law is the law of intention and desire. It states that inherent in having an intention or a desire is the ability to fulfil it. Intention is a force in nature, just as electricity and magnetism are. Remember I told you that the Rig Veda says that desire is the connection between the existent and the non-existent. Desire is the engine of creation.

I have had many desires that went unfulfilled. What am I doing wrong?

You may be doing everything wrong! If you are trying hard to fulfil your desire, if you haven't examined your choices to see whether they are karmically appropriate, if you are keeping the ego as your internal reference, then you are thwarting yourself. In the field of pure potentiality is infinite organising power. If you introduce an intention into this field, which is more powerful than anything, it will bear fruit. Experience the desire there, then let the universe handle the details.

The thought occurs to me that if my desire is a selfish and narrow desire, and if I shift my internal reference point from the ego to the self, then the desire itself might disappear.

This might happen, and you will find out what your true desires are. The law is activated by knowing what your desires are, by having the ability to experience them in the gap, and finally by surrendering them to the organising power of the field of pure potentiality.

This brings us to the sixth spiritual law, which is the law of detachment. It says that if you really want something, you have to relinquish your attachment to it.

That sounds like a paradox! How does it work?

It *is* a paradox, and this paradox comes because we have two centres of being operating in us: the spirit and the ego. The spirit is engaged in alert witnessing, and this is detachment. When you are detached, you are process-orientated rather than outcome-oriented. You have a goal, but the process is the most important thing. You say, 'I am walking this road to get somewhere, but if I don't get there is doesn't matter because this is the road I want to walk, this is the road I love.'

How can we activate this principle?

There are three principles in the practice of this law. There is the principle of uncertainty. Instead of trying to establish certainty in your life, step into the unknown. The known is like a prison, it is the willingness to surrender to the unknown that frees you. The second way is as we have discussed before: to step into the world of infinite possibilities; and the third principle is to practise present-moment awareness.

Finally, there is the seventh spiritual law, and this is the law of dharma, which we discussed before. It is the law that says that we are here to fulfil a purpose. This purpose includes two goals. The first is to express your unique talents and the second is to put that talent at the service of humanity.

How does someone discover their unique talent?

If you like, make a list of the things you like doing, the things you are good at. Every human being has a unique gift, a special talent, something they do better than anyone else. Think about the thing you do that makes you lose track of time and become lost in the moment. It doesn't have to be lofty. It can be anything—cooking, taking care of children, playing sport. When you do that thing, and use it in service to others, you will experience the exultation and the ecstasy of your own spirit, which is the goal of all goals.

This brings us to the ultimate purpose of our beings: to discover the higher self, which means to realise—not intellectually, but experientially—that you are (as Teilhard de Chardin said) not a human being with occasional spiritual experiences but a spiritual being with occasional human experiences.

We should remember and act on all of the seven spiritual laws, but it seems like a lot to think about at one time.

I often tell people to concentrate on just one law a day. Think about that law on that day, and focus your awareness on it. I think that, if we have a group of people putting their attention at once on these principles, it might cause a phase transition, an evolutionary development that will change the world. If you become familiar with these seven spiritual laws on the level of your own experience, then you start a process by which you can get anything you want. Once you have integrated the seven spiritual laws into your life, you will have an understanding of awareness, of attention and of intention.

CHAPTER 6 | *Life in the Gap*

According to Deepak the gap is the soul; the karmic software from which we create our mind, our body and our experiences of the world. It's also the space between thoughts and the womb of creation.

Deepak says, 'Nature goes to exactly the same place to create a galaxy of stars, a cluster of nebulae or a rainforest as it does to create a thought.'

So how do we reach the gap? Well, one way is through meditation.

What's one of the most valuable keys to happiness?

Spending a little time with yourself. Franz Kafka once said, 'You need not do anything. Remain sitting at your table and listen.' You don't even have to listen. Learn to become quiet and still and solitary, and the world will freely offer itself to you to be unmasked. It has no choice, it will roll in ecstasy at your feet!

Most people spend a whole lifetime with strangers. They sleep every night with a stranger and the stranger is their own self.

One way to spend time with yourself is in a state of meditation.

What is the purpose of meditation?

The purpose of meditation is to take us into the field of infinite possibilities, to go into the gap between the thoughts, then to come back here in order to create according to our dreams. The seven spiritual laws are actually the mechanics by which this can take place, effortlessly and spontaneously. People these days do meditation for all sorts of reasons, of course: to sleep better at night, to relax, to calm anxiety, or to counteract stress. Meditation will give you all these things. But its true purpose is spiritual development, and all the rest are just side effects. Meditation is a journey that takes us to our essential state.

What happens when we meditate?

One of three things can happen. You might get restless or anxious. This indicates that you need to meditate more—that you really need meditation.

Second, you may get drowsy, and even fall asleep. This means that you need more sleep! The third experience is the one you are after: you slip into the gap between your thoughts. When this happens, you might get a feeling of tingling, or vibration, or energy. That is consciousness activating *prana*.

Is that part of how desire is fulfilled?

Once you can liberate *prana* in your own body, you can motivate the universe. It is the fifth spiritual law, the law of intention and desire. To fulfil a desire, you slip into the gap, and while you are in the gap, in the silence, you release the intention. You maintain self-referral, not object referral—your internal reference point is your spirit, not your ego. Finally, you stay detached from the outcome.

I understand that yogis, who practise meditation for many years, sometimes develop extraordinary powers. Can you explain the mechanics of that?

It is simply what I have described: keeping your internal reference point as self. When I was in medical school, a yogi demonstrated that he could plunge a knife into his body without spilling a drop of blood. But he was young, and when someone in the class started making fun of him, his attention shifted back to his ego and he started to bleed. However, when he realised this, he once again let go of his ego and the bleeding stopped immediately. As we progress through higher states of consciousness by practising the seven spiritual laws, we get absolute mastery over our own lives.

Does this mean that we are in full control?

No, it doesn't mean control. What it does mean is the autonomy to create the life you want for yourself and your loved ones. Active mastery means that you deal with the toxins in your life, in whatever way they manifest themselves. I mean not just toxic food or chemicals, but also toxic relationships. It means that you no longer need the approval of others, nor do you fear their approbation. You start using relationships as a mirror, for your own evolution. You love and hate people because they are actually mirrors of yourself. When you understand that, then relationships can tell you about yourself, and help you in your own evolution. When you achieve active mastery, you don't ask, 'What's in it for me?' but, 'How can I help?' You also experience sensualness, and understand how to really enjoy yourself, and to enjoy your own sensual nature. You no longer need to judge, or to classify things as good or bad. You have present-moment awareness. You know that the past is gone, that the future is not here, and that at this moment you are free of both. This is divinity. Your behaviour becomes love-based, not fear-based, and finally, active mastery is when you begin to see the whole universe as a projection of yourself.

What type of meditation is the most effective?

There are many types of meditation. Some use visualisation, some use sound or smell, some use affirmations. These are all useful forms of meditation and can bring about healing. But they are all based on mental activity. I use a type of meditation that takes you beyond the mind, to the individual soul, and finally to the spirit, or universal consciousness. This is called Primordial Sound Meditation.

Is Primordial Sound Meditation a traditional type of meditation?

Yes, it comes from a yogic tradition in India. *Yoga* and the English word *yoke* come from the same word, meaning that which brings about union. Yoga refers to the union of the mind, the body, the soul and the spirit. At the most sublime level, at the level of the spirit, all is one, and yoga can take us to that realisation. The Yoga Sutras of Patanjali form the classic text of yoga, and the first four sutras contain the nub of all Patanjali's teachings. The first sutra simply introduces the text, but the second sutra describes yoga as 'the settling down of the mind into the field of pure silence'. The third sutra goes on to say that, when the mind is silent, then we are in our natural state—pure, unbounded spirit.

If pure silence is our natural state, why does it seem so elusive to us?

The fourth sutra answers just that question. It says that our essential state is overshadowed by the activity of the mind. Attention goes to the world, rather than to the self, and we forget our true nature. This is a disturbed state of consciousness. The pristine, undisturbed state is that of infinite stillness, infinite potentiality.

Yoga encompasses lots of *mudras,* postures, and meditative techniques. But these four sutras express the core teaching of yoga. The purpose of yoga is to get to that state, and to do it you need to get beyond the activity of the mind. In other words, you need to slip into the gap between your thoughts. Between the thoughts is the thinker.

You recommend Primordial Sound Meditation. Isn't it ironic that we use sound to get to the silence?

Remember that sound is the first code of intelligence, the first movement of consciousness. When you think something, that is also a form of hearing. We hear our thoughts, and since thinking is the most subtle form of activity, sound is the most subtle of all our experiences. The essence of sound is the primordial sound. Mantras are primordial sounds, the essence of which is pure consciousness.

Are all mantras of equal value?

There are different sorts of mantras used for different purposes: there are mantras for healing, for changing the body, for changing our surroundings. But the mantras we are talking about here are called '*bija* mantras'. *Bija* means seed. To use this mantra, you need a teacher to give it to you and to teach you how to use it.

A friend of mine was told to keep her mantra secret. Why is that?

You don't have to, you know. You can go and tell everyone if you want to. The reason you are told to keep it secret is that it becomes like a covenant or a sacrament. There is nothing to say you can't tell everyone, but I have found that people who do this, who trivialise the sacrament, don't practise it. Rituals do have a purpose, and their purpose is to grab your attention.

Can you use a mantra you get from a book?

The mantras are all there in the yoga sutras, so it isn't as if you can never find one without a teacher. But once again, unless you go through the ritual of using a teacher and receiving your own mantra, it may not be imbued with that special meaning for you. There is no punishment; it is just that you might not keep practising it.

Thoughts often intrude during meditation. How can we control this?

Don't try to control it. Say you are sitting, meditating, but at the same time, you are thinking about what to prepare for dinner tonight, about what someone said to you, about someone's birthday which you forgot. If you try to push these thoughts out, they will just get stronger. It is counterproductive. Never judge the quality of your meditation—that is, whether you are doing the mantra correctly. Once you get results you will know that you are doing it correctly. So when you become aware of the fact that you are thinking, you shift your attention back to the mantra. As you continue to do this, the thoughts become fainter and fainter, and even the mantra fades. Suddenly the thoughts disappear and the mantra also disappears. What remains is the one who witnesses and creates these thoughts. You are now in touch with your soul, with your own essential state.

Couldn't someone just make up their own mantra? Just choose a word to say? Isn't it the repetition that counts, rather than the word? Maybe we could just watch our breath.

Yes is the answer to all your questions. Alfred Lord Tennyson used to sit and say his own name over and over again. But a mantra is a reliable, proven way. Like a path that has been well trodden, it is actually easier and more efficient due to the fact that so many people have used it over the centuries. Mantras have their own morpho-genetic fields, and are universal sounds.

Are there other meditations?

Yes, there are the heart sutras, which are immensely powerful. You should have a teacher guide you through these. They are delicate and powerful, and there are twenty-eight of them. Their effects are extremely beneficial for you and for everyone around you.

Do spiritual experiences occur once we have learned how to slip into the gap?

Yes, there are seven states of consciousness. Three of them we are familiar with from our everyday experiences. The first is the state of deep sleep. The second is the state of dreams, which is more alert than deep sleep, although you have the seed of consciousness even in the state of deep sleep. Then there is the waking state, in which we look back at our dreams and realise they they are not real. It is the same with people who have experienced *atma darshan*, which is the direct experience of soul. They say that when you 'wake' into that state, you recognise that your waking state is no more real than the dream.

Atma darshan is the fourth state of consciousness, the experience of the soul. We call it non-local reality. At first that experience is just temporary, and we go back and forth, from local to non-local reality. There comes a time when that memory of our self stays with us, when eternity stays with us, even in the midst of acting in the world. We experience local and non-local reality at the same time. When you have this experience, you are in a higher state of consciousness, the fifth state of consciousness.

In the sixth state of consciousness you realise not only that you are non-local reality, but that the other person is, too—that is, you as spirit. When you see that, that I am eternal consciousness, and that we are both playing our roles in this eternal cosmic drama, you see the divinity not only in me, but in everything. This is called divine consciousness.

Finally, there is the seventh state of consciousness, in which you achieve unified consciousness. Then the divinity in you merges with the divinity in everything else. You are the universe. You are everywhere and everything.

Are there any other ways in which to reach the gap?

Well, I've always believed that poetry is a method of going into the gap. When I was a child I would listen to my grandmother read me sacred Indian myths, and these myths, with all their mystery, magic, wonder and enchantment, would entice my imagination. Later I began to recognise that all the experiences of spirituality can be learned through the poetry of Shakespeare, Tennyson, Byron, Shelley, Coleridge, Tagore, and so on.

Did this encourage you to write your own poems?

Yes. Over the years I've written verses for my own enjoyment, but recently I began to write poetry as part of a ten-week prenatal course at the center. While I was doing that, I also felt inspired by some of the things that I had previously written. All this then culminated in a book I called *Raid on the Inarticulate*.

Also, you are devoting a lot of time to adapting your work to music. You're working on a number of CDs and are incorporating your music into your seminars and workshops. Why the greater focus on music?

A lot of people do not have the capacity or desire to understand my material intellectually, but many understand it at the level of the heart. I found that, if you can give people the same knowledge through music, they relate to it. That means the knowledge becomes experiential for them. I find music to be an extremely powerful tool because people will listen to the same song even a hundred times, but don't go to the same movie (even if they love it) more than two or three times. So we respond to music in very powerful ways.

Who are you working with and what type of music can we expect to hear?

I am working with The Humming Boys, a popular US hip-hop band, and also with street music (hip-hop) to see how I can explain some of these abstract philosophical concepts in a language that people can understand.

I'm working with street poets and street artists. I am very excited about this project. I may even make music videos for television. There will be voice-overs from me in the form of speeches (shorts with insights) and then foreground music. You'll be able to dance to the music as well. People will not only learn intellectually, but will also dance to the knowledge.

You have taken us on a fascinating journey in thought. And it sounds as though all of us have the power to go on our own, even-more-fascinating journey, within ourselves.

That's right. And where you end up is where you started—it is a journey without distance. You find out that the soul is ineffable, abstract, vast, mysterious unbounded, eternal ... and yet it is more real than a rock. It is who you are.

FURTHER READING

BOOKS BY DEEPAK CHOPRA

Ageless Body, Timeless Mind

In *Ageless Body, Timeless Mind,* Deepak discusses ageing as a choice. He suggests that the body is not an object but part of a process that has no predetermined fate. The book's central theme concerns the connection between mind and body, and how this relationship affects our lives, contributing to an overall sense of well-being.

Understanding the mind-body relationship helps us to acknowledge our full potential, free from self-imposed limitations. While Deepak's concepts may seem relatively new in terms of modern-day thought, they are actually steeped in wisdom that is as old as humanity itself.

Deepak discusses an alternative to growing old that blows old age into one thousand pieces and sends it orbiting into outer space. As one of his eighty-year-old patients said, 'People don't grow old. When they stop growing, they become old.'

The Return of Merlin

As the title suggest, *The Return of Merlin* is an adaptation of one of the most fascinating and enduring myths of our time: the story of King Arthur and his kingdom, Camelot. Deepak has re-written this fabulous myth in a delightful and enthralling style. As you read you are taken to a world that seems far away yet simultaneously close. Deepak takes you on a journey from one era to the next, through the 'web of time', which is sure to open your mind to a new reality.

The Return of Merlin invites readers to reconnect with the Merlin that lies within each of us: that part of us that is all-powerful, all-seeing, eternal. As you read you are taken to a world of mystery, magic and intrigue.

In each of the characters you will identify the roles that you and those around you play subconsciously in the game of life. *The Return of Merlin* is about transcending this game and reclaiming the pure knowledge that lies hidden in the purity of our hearts.

The Way of the Wizard

The Way of the Wizard — Twenty Spiritual Lessons

for Creating the Life You Want is a guide to using spiritual alchemy in order to awaken the magic in everyday life.

In this book, Deepak uses the metaphysical themes from the well-known Merlin and Arthur myths, and highlights the importance of the wizard's world. Deepak believes we all need wizards for they help 'to lift us from the ordinary and humdrum to the kind of significance we tend to relegate to myth but which is actually right at hand here and now'.

The Way of the Wizard lists twenty principles for creating the life we want by rediscovering the magic that lies dormant within us all.

The principles in the book are accessible and within anyone's grasp. Deepak uses dialogue between the wizard Merlin and his pupil Arthur to outline each invaluable lesson. He then goes on to explain how these important codes can be applied to improve our everyday life.

In *The Way of the Wizard* the reader embarks on a journey into a realm of boundless possibilities that exists within, and all around, each of us.

Boundless Energy

In *Boundless Energy,* Deepak draws on Ayurvedic principles to present his unique approach to combating chronic fatigue syndrom (CFS).

As he explains, 'Ayurveda works on the principle that there are three distinct body types that a person may be influenced by. A person may also be a unique mixture of parts of each of these body types.'

Therefore, each of us is fundamentally unique and cannot be treated in exactly the same manner.

Boundless Energy includes a chapter designed to help you determine the body type you are and the characteristics you ascribe to.

In *Boundless Energy* you will learn how to derive more energy from food, unlock your mind's potential to produce vigour, balance your behavioural patterns with your environment, and uncover the power of personal growth.

The Seven Spiritual Laws of Success

In *The Seven Spiritual Laws of Success,* Deepak distils the essence of his teachings into seven simple yet powerful principles that can be applied to create success in all areas of your life.

According to Deepak, the book is based on natural laws that govern all of creation.

The Seven Spiritual Laws of Success offers a life-altering perspective on the attainment of success: once we understand our true nature and learn to live in harmony with natural law, a sense of well-being, good health, fulfilling relationships, energy and enthusiasm for life, and material abundance will spring forth easily and effortlessly.

This book contradicts the idea that success is the result of hard work, exacting plans or driving ambition.

Baffled? You won't be for long.

Deepak's perceptions are filled with timeless wisdom and practical steps that the reader can apply to their life immediately.

The Seven Spiritual Laws of Success is inspiring to read and a highly recommended book for positive growth.

Creating Affluence

In his opening to *Creating Affluence*, Deepak tells a tale of a spiritual master and his apprentice. The wisdom given involves the Indian Goddesses Sarasvati and Lakshmi. Sarasvati is the Goddess of Knowledge, Lakshmi the Goddess of Wealth. The lesson is: the more you seek the Goddess of Knowledge, the more the Goddess of Wealth follows you.

Creating Affluence is a beautifully presented book, each page designed with a gold-coloured leafy border, and has equally wonderful content. It's much more than simply a book on how to make money. Deepak discusses the source of all affluence, then proceeds to list alphabetically the steps to creating it. Each step contains a seed of knowledge that can be adopted in our everyday lives for growth and prosperity. The idea is to take the seed, nurture and feed it, then watch as affluence enters our life.

This book can be used as a lifetime companion, giving insight and advice during those trying times that we all experience as human beings.

Restful Sleep

If you have to endure sleepless nights, then Deepak's

book *Restful Sleep,* with practical advice and insightful research, is the perfect guide. The main focus is on nature. According to Deepak, the more in tune you are with nature's rhythms, the easier it is to have a restful night's sleep.

Modern society is removed from nature's cycles, which ultimately interferes with our sleep cycle. Deepak suggests that the first step to a better night's sleep is establishing a routine.

From this basic premise, Deepak shows how you can enjoy restful sleep without tranquillisers, how to wake feeling rested and how to deal with an overactive mind at bedtime. Steeped in Ayurvedic literature, *Restful Sleep* is full of helpful tips and thoughtful knowledge.

Perfect Weight

Weight seems to be a topic on every woman's lips, and many men's too. No matter how much we weigh, many of us simply aren't happy with our body size. We're either too fat or too thim, but rarely do we describe ourselves as just right.

In *Perfect Weight,* Deepak helps readers to reach their ideal weight without having to experience tiresome dieting regimes or exercise programs. The basic premise is 'Eat whenever you are hungry; but when you're not hungry, don't eat.'

After you've got your mind firmly around this, Deepak goes on to explain the importance of recognising your Ayurvedic body type and how to determine it. Once you know your body type, you'll be able to discern certain characteristics about yourself, including your essential body shape and size. For many people this involves accepting a body shape that isn't necessarily the ideal that is represented in the media and women's magazines. After all, this book is about reaching *your* ideal weight, not someone else's.

With easy-to-follow tips and ideas, Deepak offers readers a book that is practical and enlightening.

Perfect Health

In this book Deepak discusses the 5000-year-old Indian medical system called Ayurveda. Based on an individual's body type, important information is shared regarding diet, exercise, daily routines and stress reduction.

In an age where good health is constantly reiterated, Deepak offers insightful hints on how to achieve and maintain a healthy disposition.

Deepak shows you how to restore balance in your life by learning to really listen to your body's needs, and distinguishing these from its wants. *Perfect Health* is about knowing yourself. Once you've achieved this, you'll be able to use Deepak's additional advice to determine what is beneficial and what is not so beneficial for your body type.

Perfect Health—The Complete Mind/Body Guide will provide insights into achieving optimum well-being.

Perfect Digestion

Proper digestion is the cornerstone of good health: if you don't have a well-functioning digestive system then the healthiest foods in the world aren't going to benefit you. It's important to recognise this, and it's equally important to have a fair idea about how digestion and the elimination processes function. To help you better understand, Deepak has explained everything in *Perfect Digestion*.

Deepak's techniques and insights are based on the Ayurvedic tradition which takes into consideration not only the physical aspects of health but the emotional aspects as well. If you have any problems whatsoever associated with your digestive system, including irritable bowel syndrome, constipation, diarrhoea or gaseousness, then you'll find helpful guidance within the pages of *Perfect Digestion*.

Unconditional Life

In an uplifting, frank and entertaining way, Deepak explains in *Unconditional Life* the power of individual consciousness. Through personal anecdote, Deepak recounts the episodes that occurred in his own life which challenged his beliefs and led him on a path of uncovering his own unique power— a power that resides within all of us and enables each and every one of us to fulfil our dreams.

Unconditional Life examines the notion that we can influence our reality purely through our thoughts. Deepak shows that it certainly does seem to be that way, as long as we combine modern scientific thought with ancient wisdom. The result is an illuminating book that can be read with ease while prompting much thought and interest.

Raid on the Inarticulate

Raid on the Inarticulate is a collection of poems by Deepak, incorporating his vast wisdom and insight. This book is for people with a penchant for poetry, especially its beautiful rhythms and metaphors.

Deepak has long had an interest in reading poetry, and savouring its magic and its ability to touch a person's heart rather than simply their mind. Deepak believes poetry allows us to 'slip into the gap between our thoughts and get in touch with the karmic software of our souls'. To enter such a world of enchantment, read this book.

The Path to Love

There are few universal threads in life as intrinsic as love. Its murmurings can be heard in all corners of the globe. Yet while we may talk of love, we have different ideas about what it is. In his book *The Path to Love,* Deepak explores 'spiritual' love: a love that takes the individual to ecstasy.

The Path to Love provides an insightful glimpse into attraction, infatuation, courtship, intimacy, attachment and passion. Based on ancient Indian knowledge, it gives the reader a unique opportunity to reach beyond Earth-bound notions of love to a spiritual understanding. No longer will love be seen as something that can suddenly be taken away. Instead, you will see it as eternal and all-encompassing, something that accompanies you throughout life, providing a constant.

Quantum Healing

Quantum Healing—Exploring the Frontiers of Mind/Body Medicine is for anyone interested in achieving or maintaining optimum health. It may be of special interest to those suffering from serious illness.

Deepak has a wonderful ability to relate seemingly complex material in an easy-to-read format. In *Quantum Healing* he expands on the notion that healing is not simply a physical process but a mental one also. He discusses the quantum mechanical body and Ayurveda, and dedicates a chapter to the 'birth of disease'.

In an age in which more people are developing deep respect for natural medicine, Deepak offers an in-depth and insightful guide using both medical science and Eastern philosophy.

The Seven Spiritual Laws of Parents

In response to the phenomenal bestseller, *The Seven Spiritual Laws of Success,* Deepak has released a book especially for parents, giving insight into the spirituality of child rearing. The book is designed to help parents share with their children the value of spirituality as well as the experience of abundance.

The Seven Spiritual Laws for Parents moves beyond the notions of 'good' or 'bad' parenting to a place where the whole family can enjoy the spiritual nature of communion with family.

Deepak has also produced a number of audio and video cassettes covering all aspects of his teachings.

BOOKS BY LEON NACSON

I Must Be Dreaming

You don't have to wait for your dreams to come true—they are! *I Must Be Dreaming* provides readers with a simple guide to dream interpretation.

Written in a fluid style and sprinkled with humorous asides, this book covers everything from how to get a good night's sleep to how to create your own dream dictionary.

If you're fascinated by your dreams but are unsure of their origins or even their purpose, this is the perfect book to read as an introduction to one of the most fascinating aspects of our lives.

This book allows readers to explore their world of dreams, offering guidance and awareness that can be extended for use in their everyday lives.

Aromatherapy for Lovers and Dreamers

co-authored by Karen Downes and Judith White

Aromatherapy for Lovers and Dreamers will appeal to the lover and dreamer in all of us. Loving and dreaming are two aspects of life most of us enjoy. This book is designed to heighten these areas of enjoyment using the power of aromatherapy. Every facet of loving and dreaming is covered, including how to attract a dream lover, how to give your real lover an erotic massage and which oils to use to make your underwear just a splash more special. *Aromatherapy for Lovers and Dreamers* provides readers with practical steps they can take to make their dream and love lives more blissful.

Aromatherapy for Meditation and Contemplation

co-authored by Karen Downes and Judith White

Meditation and contemplation often provide us with much needed time to devise great ideas and endeavours, giving us the courage and faith to step forward. *Aromatherapy for Meditation and Contemplation* explores meditation and contemplation, discussing them in great detail and linking each with the world of aromatherapy for positive life direction.

With a detailed exposition on how the brain works, including information on the power of smell, *Aromotherapy for Meditation and Contemplation* presents information that is informative and practical for this age of fast-paced living and achieving.

Dyer Straight

Within the covers of *Dyer Straight*, the reader will find straight answers from Wayne Dyer on personal growth, self-help, relationships, abundance, and how to create miracles for yourself. Wayne reveals the keys to gaining heightened awareness; insights into his personal life; and why he journeyed into the personal growth arena.

Wayne Dyer and Leon Nacson are friends and colleagues. Over a period of five years, Leon managed to get answers to the questions most often asked on Wayne Dyer. The responses are in this book.

Cards, Stars and Dreams
co-authored by Matthew Favaloro

Cards, Stars and Dreams is a combination of three great intuitive sciences—tarot, astrology and dreams. The practical nature of this book means anyone can use it to find inner guidance. The fundamental theme of the book is self-help. Rather than provide information on how to use tarot reading, dream interpretation and astrology to help other people in their life journey, *Cards, Stars and Dreams* was specifically written with the individual in mind, as a manual for personal growth. Various techniques are described on how to use these three intuitive sciences to determine for yourself the way that best helps you to find inner harmony and direction.

Simply Wilde

Simply Wilde is an entertaining journey inside the mind of one of today's foremost self-help authors, Stuart Wilde. People have often pondered the mystery behind Wilde, this prominent and controversial figure in the human potential movement. Here, for the first time, Stuart candidly answers questions that give rare insight into his opinions, thoughts, feelings, hopes and dreams. He explores issues in which we all share an interest, and deals with dilemmas many of us face in life. This collection of captivating perceptions makes *Simply Wilde* reading.

Deepak Chopra and The Chopra Center for Well Being in La Jolla, California, offer a wide range of seminars, products and educational programmes worldwide. The Chopra Center offers revitalizing mind/body programmes, as well as day spa services. Guests can come to rejuvenate, expand knowledge or obtain a medical consultation.

For information on meditation classes, health and well-being courses, instructor certification programmes, or local classes in your area, contact The Chopra Center for Well Being, 7630 Fay Avenue, La Jolla, California, 92037, USA. By telephone: 001-888-424-6772, or 001-619-551-7788. For a virtual tour of the Center, visit the Internet website at www.chopra.com.

To receive a complimentary issue of Dr. Chopra's monthly newsletter, Infinite Possibilities for Body, Mind & Soul, or to subscribe, call 001-800-829-3356. You may also write c/o Deepak Chopra's Infinite Possibilities for Body, Mind & Soul, P.O. Box 420051, Palm Coast, FL 32142-0051, USA.

For more information about Dr. Chopra's books and audiotapes, visit http://www.randomhouse.com/site/chopra.

If you live in Europe and would like more information on workshops, lectures or other programmes about Dr. Deepak Chopra or to order any of his books, tapes or products, please contact: Contours, 44 Fordbridge Road, Ashford, Middlesex, TW15 2SJ (tel: +44 (0) 181 564 7033; fax: +44 (0) 181 897 3807).

Also available from Rider Books:

WAYNE DYER
How to manifest your heart's desires

Leon Nacson

As one of the most inspiring teachers of the present time, Wayne Dyer has helped millions to new levels of self-awareness – and sold over 48 million books around the world.

In this enlightening work, his friend and colleague, Leon Nacson, asks the questions so many have wanted to ask Dr Dyer over the last few years, on personal growth, self-help, relationships, abundance and creating miracles.

This book is essential reading for anyone wanting to hear the full message of the 'Father of Motivation' – and to change their life.

If you would like to order any of the following books or to receive our catalogue please fill in the form below:

By Deepak Chopra

Ageless Body, Timeless Mind	£7.99
Restful Sleep	£7.99
Perfect Weight	£8.99
Perfect Digestion	£7.99
Boundless Energy	£7.99
Journey Into Healing	£8.99
The Way of the Wizard	£9.99
The Path to Love	£9.99
Overcoming Addictions	£7.99
Healing the Heart	£7.99
The Love Poems of Rumi (ed.)	£6.99

Wayne Dyer: How to manifest your heart's desires
   by Leon Nacson   £5.99

HOW TO ORDER

BY POST: TBS Direct, TBS Ltd, Colchester Road, Frating Green, Essex CO7 7DW

Please send me _____ copies of   @ £   each

☐ I enclose my cheque for £ _____ payable to Rider Books

☐ Please charge £ _____ to my American Express/Visa/Mastercard account*

   (*delete as applicable)

Card No ☐☐☐☐☐☐☐☐☐☐☐☐☐☐☐☐☐☐☐

Expiry Date: ☐☐☐☐   Signature _____

Name _____

Address _____

_____ Postcode _____

Delivery address if different _____

_____ Postcode _____

Or call our credit card hotline on 01206 255800.
Please have your card details handy
Please quote reference ChopraNacson

    Rider is an imprint of Random House UK Ltd

Please tick here if you do not wish to receive further information from Rider or associated companies ☐